BY WENDELL BERRY

FICTION

The Discovery of Kentucky
Fidelity
The Memory of Old Jack
Nathan Coulter
A Place on Earth
Remembering
Watch With Me
The Wild Birds

POETRY

Clearing
Collected Poems: 1957–1982
The Country of Marriage
Entries
Farming: A Hand Book
Openings
A Part
Sabbaths
Sayings and Doings
Traveling at Home
The Wheel

ESSAYS

A Continuous Harmony
The Gift of Good Land
Harland Hubbard: Life and Work
The Hidden Wound
Home Economics
Recollected Essays: 1965–1980
Sex, Economy, Freedom & Community
Standing by Words
The Unforeseen Wilderness
The Unsettling of America
What Are People For?

The
Hidden
Wound

·

Wendell
Berry

North Point Press

Farrar, Straus and Giroux
New York

The author is grateful to New Directions Publishing Corporation for permission to quote from the following: "Salutation" by Ezra Pound, from *Personae*, copyright 1926 by Ezra Pound. *Confucius* by Ezra Pound, copyright 1928 by Glenn Hughes, copyright 1947 by Ezra Pound. "The Poor" by William Carlos Williams, from *Collected Earlier Poems*, copyright 1938 by William Carlos Williams. "Pere Sebastian Rasles" by William Carlos Williams, from *In the American Grain*, copyright 1925 by James Laughlin, copyright 1933 by William Carlos Williams.

The publisher wishes to thank the Pace trust of Louisville, Kentucky, for its assistance in the publication of this volume.

LIBRARY OF CONGRESS
CATALOGING-IN-PUBLICATION DATA
Berry, Wendell, 1934–
    The hidden wound/Wendell Berry.
        p.   cm.
    Reprint. Originally published: Boston: Houghton
    Mifflin, 1970. With new afterword.
    1. United States—Race relations   2. Southern States—
    Race relations.   3. Afro-Americans—Social conditions—
    1964–1975.   4. Afro-Americans—Southern States—
    Social conditions.   I. Title.
    E185.61B46   1989
    305.8'96073—dc19
                                            88-34555

North Point Press
A division of Farrar, Straus and Giroux
New York

In memory of
Nick Watkins
&
Aunt Georgie Ashby

But I want to tell you something. This pattern, this "system" that the white man created, of teaching Negroes to hide the truth from him behind a facade of grinning, "yessir-bossing," foot-shuffling and head-scratching—that system has done the American white man more harm than an invading army would do to him.   *The Autobiography of Malcolm X*

. . . wanting good government in their own states, they first established order in their own families; wanting order in the home, they first disciplined themselves; desiring self-discipline, they rectified their own hearts; and wanting to rectify their hearts, they sought precise verbal definitions of their inarticulate thoughts (the tones given off by the heart) . . .

Confucius, *The Great Digest* (translated by Ezra Pound)

. . . I am—the brutal thing itself.

William Carlos Williams, *In the American Grain*

The Hidden Wound

· *I* ·

It occurs to me that, for a man whose life from the beginning has been conditioned by the lives of black people, I have had surprisingly little to say about them in my other writings. Perhaps this is justifiable—there is certainly no requirement that a writer deal with any particular subject—and yet it has been an avoidance. When I have written about them before I have felt that I was doing little more than putting down a mark, leaving an opening, that I would later have to go back to and fill. For whatever reasons, good or bad, I have been unwilling until now to open in myself what I have known all along to be a wound—a historical wound, prepared centuries ago to come alive in me at my birth like a hereditary disease, and to be augmented and deepened by my life. If I had thought it was only the black people who have suffered from the years of slavery and racism, then I could have dealt fully with the matter long ago; I could have filled myself with pity for them, and would no doubt have enjoyed it a great deal and thought highly of myself. But I am sure it is not so simple as that. If white people have suffered less obviously from racism than black people, they have nevertheless suffered greatly; the cost has been greater perhaps than we can yet know. If the white man has inflicted the wound of racism upon black men, the cost has been that he would receive the mirror image of that wound into himself. As the master, or as a member of the dominant race, he has felt little compulsion to acknowledge it or speak of it; the more painful it has grown the more deeply he has hidden it within himself. But the wound is there, and it is a profound disorder, as great a damage in his mind as it is in his society.

This wound is in me, as complex and deep in my flesh as blood and nerves. I have borne it all my life, with varying degrees of consciousness, but always carefully, always with the most delicate consideration for the pain I would feel if I were somehow forced to acknowledge it. But now I am increasingly aware of the opposite compulsion. I want to know, as fully and exactly as I can, what the wound is and how much I am suffering from it. And I want to be cured; I want to be free of the wound myself, and I do not want to pass it on to my children. Perhaps this is only wishful thinking; perhaps such a thing is not to be done by one man, or in one generation. Surely a man would have to be almost dangerously proud to think himself capable of it. And so maybe I am really saying only that I feel an obligation to make the attempt, and that I know if I fail to make at least the attempt I forfeit any right to hope that the world will become better than it is now.

· 2 ·

Stories that have come down to me tell me that on both sides of my family there were slaveholders. And it is probably of some importance to try to say exactly how these stories were handed down. It would be easy to allow the impression that the past and its assumptions were deliberately and consciously planted in my mind by my elders. But that is not at all the way it was. The various households of my family were always visiting back and forth, and I spent a lot of time as a child listening to the grownups' talk—the ever-circling patterns of *reminding* that carried their thoughts from the present to the past. Some stories were repeated many times; because there was much shared knowledge, nobody would have thought of objecting to the retelling of a well-known story. This repetition of what was known in common, I think, was a sort of ritualization of the family's awareness of itself as a unit holding together through time. Among these stories there were a good many memories of slavery, casually told and heard, usually without comment beyond the facts of the narrative. What interests me about them now is that they were not forgotten, and that they were remembered and retold *casually*. For years that was the way I knew them—casually. They interested me, as the other stories did, because of the sense of the past I got from them. But the moral strain in them never reached me until some years after I had become a man. There is a peculiar tension in the casualness of this hereditary knowledge of hereditary evil; once it begins to be released, once you begin to awaken to the realities of what you know, you are subject to staggering recognitions of your complicity in history and in the events of your own life. The truth keeps leaping on you from behind. For me, that my people had owned slaves once seemed merely a curious fact. Later, I think, I took it to prove that I was somehow special, being thus associated with a historical scandal. It took me a long time, and in fact a good deal of effort, to finally realize that in owning slaves my ancestors assumed limitations and implicated themselves in troubles that have lived on to afflict me—and I still bear that knowledge with a sort of astonishment.

The most troubling of the stories I remember hearing is about the sale of a slave. It is not the sort of story that a family could remember gladly; mine has remembered it, I think, because it is too painful to forget. My great-grandfather, John Johnson Berry, once owned a slave who was a "mean nigger," too defiant and rebellious to do anything with. And writing that down, I sense as I never have before the innate violence of the slave system, and the innate flaw of the slavery myth. For if there was any kindness in slavery it was dependent on the docility of the slaves; any slave who was *unwilling* to be a slave broke through the myth of paternalism and benevolence, and brought down on himself the violence inherent in the system. A slave was obviously not a neighbor whom one could either associate with or ignore; so long as he remained docile (and indispensable) he was, as the myth would have it, a sort of stepchild whom the white master fed and clothed, and ruled and used. But a slave who was rebellious and mean obviously had to be dealt with, and the method of dealing with him had to be violent: the master had either to answer the slave's violence with greater violence of his own, or to invoke the institutional violence of slavery, selling the slave to someone more able or willing than himself to enact the necessary cruelty. My great-grandfather was evidently a rather mild and gentle man by nature, and he lived in a country of relatively small farms where domestic violence would have been very noticeable and disruptive. Unwilling for these reasons to commit personal violence against his slave, he was forced to accept the institutional violence as a sort of refuge. He sold the slave to a local slave buyer by the name of Bart Jenkins.

And here the necessary moral complicity of the slave owners in the evil of slavery becomes inescapably clear. In spite of the self-defensive myth of benevolence, it was impossible for the slave owner to secure any limit to the depth or the extent of his complicity; as soon as he found it necessary to deal with the slave as property he was in as deep as he could go. In the commercial and legal aspect of slavery the moral interest is completely crowded out and replaced by the machinery of economics: to sell a man is to abandon him. Once the contract is signed, he is as utterly beyond reach and beyond help as if buried alive. Having completed his purchase, Bart Jenkins came in the night, and knocked the man on the head while he was asleep, and bound him, and led him away with a rope.

I find it impossible to believe that my great-grandfather and his household were resigned or oblivious to the pain in this. I am fairly sure that it shocked and grieved them, and left them deeply disturbed. The farm would have had only a few slaves; association with them would have been constant and close; for life to have been bearable in such a situation there would have had to be a certain amiability between the white family and the slaves. My ancestor, as I have said, was a mild sort of man; there is, in fact, a story that he was thought too kind to his slaves, always insisting that they rest after dinner before going back to work in the afternoon. It is easy for me to imagine a profound sickness of heart permeating the life of the farm for weeks after the sale of that slave and Bart Jenkins's brutal taking of possession. No one could have *wanted* any such thing to happen. Far from that, I don't think they even *expected* any such thing to happen. They were burdened with a malignant history and a malignant inheritance, and they endeavored to protect themselves by a carefully contrived myth, preserving them against any acknowledgment, spoken or unspoken, of their involvement. I don't think they expected the slave to be rebellious; I think it is even possible that my great-grandfather did not understand, in any way that he would have acknowledged to himself beforehand, that in selling the slave he abandoned him to violence. It seems quite possible that Bart Jenkins appeared to the white household that night, to their astonishment, as the agent of a horror and an outrage that they had inherited and lived with all their lives, and had never openly faced.

I think that may be why the story was remembered: it was an eruption of something painful and threatening through the familiar even surface of their life—something they had to recognize as having been always potential, ready to spring upon them out of their inherited and meticulously preserved blindness to what slavery meant to slaves, and to masters as well. But the recognition did not accompany the story as it was handed down. I feel in the story as it has been told to me a peculiar muteness, which I now know has followed me through all my life; it is the silence with which white men in this country have surrounded the anguish implicit in their racism. The story has passed from generation to generation in flight from its horror. It has been told and retold, surely, because in the depths of our souls we all have recognized in it an evil that is native to us and that we cannot escape. Probably it has also been told as a confession, in the unspoken, even the unthought, hope that we will finally tell it to someone who can forgive us. But its pain has never been openly admitted into it. It has come down casually, posing as a bit of interesting history; I have told it that way many times myself. And so the wound has lived beneath the skin.

———

There is a good deal more to be told about the slave buyer, Bart Jenkins. As it happens, he is a figure of a certain historical prominence, one of the many heroes of a book entitled *Kentucky Cavaliers in Dixie* by George Dallas Mosgrove. This is a history of the Confederate Fourth Kentucky Cavalry Regiment, which for a time belonged to the division commanded by General John Hunt Morgan. The book was first published in 1895 and was reissued in 1957. Aside from its considerable value as a record of events, *Kentucky Cavaliers in Dixie* is interesting for its diction and style. As the title implies, it was written under the spell of chivalry and medieval romance. In his Preface, Mosgrove introduces himself in this way: ". . . I was living in Hunters Bottom, on the banks of La Belle Riviere, near Carrollton, Ky., when I mounted a charger and rode to Dixieland to serve her cause . . ."

There are passages in which he describes the inhumanity and carnage of the war unflinchingly, in clear detail, as in his account of the Battle of Saltville:

> With their long-range Enfield rifles the Fourth Kentucky made many a Federal bite the dust, and they guyed and tantalized the wavering, dispirited boys in blue unmercifully. They would fire a volley and then yell, "Come right up and draw your salt!" Silas Sims, a dead-shot, would draw a bead on a blue-coat, blaze away and then hail the "yank" with the interrogatory, "How's that; am I shooting too high

or too low?" Afterward, while passing over the field, Sims came upon the body of a dead officer whose head had been partially torn away by a cannon ball. The unsympathetic Confederate, with grim humor, took a handful of salt from his haversack and threw it into the cavity in the dead officer's head, saying, "There, you came for salt, now take some."

But he appears only to have to raise his head a little from such scenes to imagine himself and his comrades involved in a pageant of gallantry, tournaments, and jousts. The language thus involves a sort of schizophrenia, a curious ability to confront the most horrible facts and then to look away from them, as if they did not exist, into a medieval fantasy. And the medieval fantasy is sometimes ornamented with Napoleonic fantasy.

It is in his account of General Humphrey Marshall's staff officers—"intrepid, efficient, accomplished gentlemen and soldiers"— that Mosgrove first speaks of "the conspicuous figure of Captain Bart W. Jenkins, the tall, dashing, impulsive aide-de-camp, brave as Marshal Lannes . . ."

Jenkins's service as a staff officer apparently ended in the spring of 1863, when General Marshall resigned his commission. From then until the end of the war Jenkins led a company of free-lancers, and it is in this role that he figures most prominently in Mosgrove's book. The nineteenth chapter, in fact, is titled "Captain Bart W. Jenkins and His Troopers," and it carries this epigraph:

> He was a stalworth knight and keen,
> And had in many a battle been;
> His eyebrow dark and eye of fire,
> Showed spirit proud and prompt to ire;
> Yet lines of thought upon his cheek,
> Did deep design and counsel speak.

In thinking of those lines and of the following romanticized paragraphs, it should be borne in mind that highly mobile troops of free-lancers such as Jenkins led traveled light and lived off the country, and however they may have benefited the army, they were the scourge of the local populations at whose expense they lived:

> Captain Jenkins was naturally a leader, never a follower of men. He usually managed to keep his gallant troop independent and free from entanglements with other battalions. His little command, however, was . . . gladly received in any camp and their banner greeted with joyous acclaim on the battlefield,
>
> > For they were clansmen, bold and true,
> > Their chief as brave as Roderick Dhu.
>
> Captain Jenkins, always alert and a free rover, headed his horse in the direction of the enemy's guns, often dropping into a fight unexpectedly, but at an opportune time.

And then to prove "this superb cavalier's dauntless courage" we are given an incident which is probably every bit as spectacular as Mosgrove thought it was:

> Before [his?] leaving Kentucky for Dixieland a detachment of Federals, probably a company of "Home Guards," led by a United States provost marshal, undertook to arrest him near his home in Henry County. They were well armed and boasted of their prowess and determination to capture the haughty and fiery Southron. Captain Jenkins made no effort to elude them. On the contrary, while the Federals were drawn up in line for some purpose, the gallant Jenkins, unattended, suddenly appeared on the scene, and with his bridle [reins] in his teeth and a revolver in each hand he deliberately rode the full length of the enemy's line. He uttered no word, but his cool audacity and his flashing eyes effectually quelled the Home Guardian war spirit—not a man of them daring to molest him.

And finally, toward the end of the book, we read:

> Captain Bart Jenkins and a number of other officers were asleep in
> Abingdon when the Federals entered the town. Captain Jenkins was
> captured successively by two soldiers. He killed both of them and es-
> caped from the town.

To round out my sketch of Captain Jenkins I will add one more
story about him, this one, like that of the slave, having come down
to me by word of mouth. My father's father remembered that when
he was a boy he once saw Bart Jenkins in a heated argument with
another man; the two were standing on the sidewalk in the town of
New Castle, the county seat of Henry County. Bart Jenkins was a
man of striking looks, correct and gentlemanly in dress and bear-
ing; he wore an immaculate pair of gray kid gloves. As the argument
went on, he worked delicately at the fingertips of one of the gloves,
as though preparing to remove it. Looking the other man levelly in
the eye, not raising his voice but speaking slowly and with precise
emphasis, working at the fingers of that glove, he said: "I wish I had
a shovel full of shit. I would throw it in your God-damned face."

· *3* ·

What I know of Captain Jenkins, then, has come to me by way of two radically different kinds of language. One, the language of spoken reminiscence—a casual, yet also apparently compulsive pondering over what happened—conveys the facts in what I suppose to be their full harshness. The other, the polite cultivated mythologizing language of Mosgrove—self-consciously public and "historical"—conveys the facts at least somewhat as they were, but always with the implied judgment that they were altogether acceptable, accommodating them within the chivalric prototype of "gentleman and soldier."

Though I have no way of proving it, I believe that it is altogether likely that Bart Jenkins was prepared for his role in the war—the reckless indulgence in violence which Mosgrove likes to think of as "dashing"—by his willing involvement in the violence of slavery. But just as Mosgrove comes nowhere near admitting that Jenkins's violence was not a violence of necessity but a violence of character, and of the crudest sort, he also never mentions that this "stalworth knight" had served his apprenticeship in the slave trade. Indeed, despite his claims that he is writing history, Mosgrove's book gives no inkling that the war occurred within a social and political context. To him it was a brilliant adventure, remote from place and time, detached from cause and effect.

One could no doubt speculate endlessly (and perhaps uselessly) as to whether this was the cause or the result of the book's chivalric conventions and gentlemanly rhetoric, but there *is* a relation. I have already said enough, I think, to make clear the profound moral discomfort potential in a society ostensibly Christian and democratic and genteel, but based upon the institutionalized violence of slavery. Though he no doubt represented a minority, Bart Jenkins was not an anomaly in that society; he served one of its designated functions, and his mentality and behavior were therefore characteristic. His fellow citizens had to contend with him as a reflection of something in themselves, and short of attempting to change the society, they had to try to live as painlessly as possible with the harsh truth that he represented. Their solution was to romanticize him. Since he was indelibly a man of violence, the only ideal figure at all close to him was that of the knight, the archetypical "gentleman and soldier." Once this mythology was accepted, the moral ground could be safely preempted by rhetoric. And so we arrive at the language of *Kentucky Cavaliers in Dixie*—a poeticized, romanticized, ornamental gentlemanly speech, so inflated with false sentiment as to sail lightly over all discrepancies in logic or in fact, shrugging off what it cannot accommodate, blandly affirming what it cannot shrug off.

If the private language of family memory has conveyed what we know to have been true of ourselves but have not admitted or judged, then the public language of Mosgrove (and many others) conveys what we *wish* had been true. Between them they define the lack of a critical self-knowledge that would offer the hope of change. This lack is the historical and psychological vacuum in which the Walt Disney version of American history was not only possible but inevitable. To my mind Disney is nothing more than a slicked-out, commercial version of Mosgrove. As a people, we have been tolled farther and farther away from the facts of what we have done by the romanticizers, whose bait is nothing more than the wishful insinuation that we have done no harm. Speaking a public language of propaganda, uninfluenced by the real content of our history which we know only in a deep and guarded privacy, we are still in the throes of the paradox of the "gentleman and soldier."

However conscious it may have been, there is no doubt in my mind that all this moral and verbal obfuscation is intentional. Nor do I doubt that its purpose is to shelter us from the moral anguish implicit in our racism—an anguish that began, deep and mute, in the minds of Christian democratic freedom-loving owners of slaves.

Another interesting example of this sort of confusion used as moral insulation is to be found in the very fabric of the liberalism of early Kentucky. Niels Henry Sonne, in *Liberal Kentucky, 1780–1828*, points out that the Kentuckians of that time supported all the principles of religious freedom, but gave their most fervid support to that of the separation of church and state. Political power was denied to practicing clergymen by the constitutions of 1792 and 1799, and it was not until 1843 that prayers were permitted to be said on any regular basis at the sessions of the legislature. According to Sonne, one of the immediate reasons for this was "the clergy's insistence upon attacking the institution of slavery." And so beneath the public advocacy of the separation of church and state, an essential of religious liberty, we see working a mute anxiety to suppress within the government of the state such admonitory voices as might discomfort the practice of slavery. For separation of church and state, then, read separation of morality and state.

From other stories that have been handed down to me I know that my people, like many others in the slave states, went to church with their slaves, were baptized with them, and presumably expected to associate with them in heaven. Again, I have been years realizing what this means, and what it has cost.

First, consider the moral predicament of the master who sat in church with his slaves, thus attesting his belief in the immortality of the souls of people whose bodies he owned and used. He thus placed his body, if not his mind, at the very crux of the deepest contradiction of his life. How could he presume to own the body of a man whose soul he considered as worthy of salvation as his own? To keep this question from articulating itself in his thoughts and demanding an answer, he had to perfect an empty space in his mind, a silence, between heavenly concerns and earthly concerns, between body and spirit. If there had ever opened a conscious connection between the two claims, if the two sides of his mind had ever touched, it would have been like building a fire in a house full of gunpowder: somewhere down deep in his mind he always knew of the danger, and his nerves were always alert to it.

But also consider this congregation of masters and slaves from the point of view of the pulpit. How, facing that mixture, and dependent on the white half of it for your livelihood, would you handle such a text as the Sermon on the Mount? It would be very desirable, and very *practical*, to preach to slaves such imperatives as these:

> . . . resist not evil: but whosoever shall smite thee on thy right cheek, turn to him the other also.

> Love your enemies, bless them that curse you, do good to them that hate you, and pray for them which despitefully use you, and persecute you . . .

Lay not up for yourselves treasures upon earth . . .

. . . all things whatsoever ye would that men should do to you, do ye
even so to them . . .

But what about the masters? Will they stand to be told such things
in the very presence of the most damning evidence against them?

Or could you even acknowledge the existence of such passages as
these from the First Epistle of John?

He that saith, I know him, and keepeth not his commandments, is a
liar, and the truth is not in him.

But whoso hath this world's good, and seeth his brother have need,
and shutteth up his bowels of compassion from him, how dwelleth
the love of God in him? My little children, let us not love in word, neither in tongue, but in deed and in truth.

If a man say I love God, and hateth his brother, he is a liar . . .

Clearly, it would not do. If a man wanted to remain a preacher he
would have to honor that division in the minds of the congregation
between earth and heaven, body and soul. His concern obviously
had to be with things heavenly; unless he was a saint or a fool he
would leave earthly things to the care of those who stood to benefit
from them.

Thus the moral obligation was cleanly excerpted from the religion. The question of how best to live on the earth, among one's fellow creatures, was permitted to atrophy, and the churches devoted
themselves exclusively and obsessively with the question of salvation.

How do you get to heaven? Well, I have quoted some passages,
and there are many others, that say you get there by obeying the
moral imperatives of the Scripture, by loving one another "in deed
and in truth." But the churches, with their strong ties to the pock-
etbooks of racists, felt obliged to see it another way: the way to

heaven was faith; one got there by *believing*. And to this day that
continues to be the emphasis of such denominations as the Southern Baptist: to be saved, believe! The mystical aspects of Christian-
ity completely overshadow the moral. But it is a bogus mysticism,
mysticism as wishful magic, a recipe by which to secure the benefits
of eternal bliss without having to give up the benefits of temporal
vice: corrupt your soul and save it too! The favorite texts of such
churches are John 3:16:

> For God so loved the world, that he gave his only begotten Son, that
> whosoever believeth in Him should not perish, but have everlasting
> life.

and Acts 16:31:

> Believe on the Lord Jesus Christ, and thou shalt be saved . . .

I have heard these passages quoted with obsessive reiteration all my
life. When the ministers of these churches turned their attention to
the world, they did so with the puritanical passion of St. Paul, vio-
lently opposing such "sins" as drinking, failure to attend church,
and "immorality"—sins of somewhat questionable status in the
first place, and which the church found it easy enough both to con-
demn and to live with, and to the practice of which its condemnation added little more than a certain spice. The great moral tasks of
honesty and peace and neighborliness and brotherhood and the
care of the earth have been left to be taken up on the streets by the
"alienated" youth of the 1960s and 1970s.

Detached from real issues and real evils, the language of religion
became abstract, intensely (desperately?) pious, rhetorical, inflated
with phony mysticism and joyless passion. The religious institutions became comfort stations for scribes and publicans and phar-
isees. Far from curing the wound of racism, the white man's Chris-

tianity has been its soothing bandage—a bandage masquerading as Sunday clothes, for the wearing of which one expects a certain moral credit.

———

By what I have said so far I have hoped to suggest some of the historical and psychological forces that shaped my native language. It was a language that clearly had developed in the presence of Negroes who once had been slaves and who now were servants. Moreover, it was a language developed in an area of small farms, where whites and Negroes worked and dealt together with some intimacy. Within the context of prejudice and segregation, the two races had to get along, and so there was an etiquette of speech that one learned from the cradle: one "respected the feelings" of Negroes, when in their presence one did not flaunt one's "superiority" or use the word *nigger*, one called elderly Negroes Aunt and Uncle, and so on. But more important, *within* the language there was a silence, an emptiness, of exactly the shape of the humanity of the black man; the language I spoke in my childhood and youth was in that way analogous to a mold in which a statue is to be cast. The options, then, were that one could, by a careful observance of the premises of the language, keep the hollow empty and thus avoid the pain of the recognition of the humanity of an oppressed people and of one's own guilt in their oppression; or one could, willing or not, be forced by the occasions of sympathy and insight to break out of those premises into a speech of another and more particular order, so that the hollow begins to fill with the substance of a life that one must recognize as human and demanding.

It seems to me that for most of my life I have been involved in the filling out of this hollow, or this silence, both unconsciously and consciously, both unwillingly and willingly. It has been laborious and painful; it has been a long process, distressingly long, and I am nowhere near the end; it may well be that I will never make it to the end. But as a part of the labor, I would like now to try to trace out how this process has occurred in me so far.

Because of the speed of change in these times, the Civil War and slavery seem as remote from us now as ancient history. In terms of the development of human events in this century a hundred years is a very long time, but in terms of the development of human minds it is not long at all. The thirty-four years of my life span an incredible amount of history: the Depression and three major wars, to name only the largest events. Though I have lived so short a time I have witnessed the advent of perhaps *most* of the forces that now condition the life of the world: the atomic bomb, television, the megalopolis, massive destruction and pollution of the environment, automation, etc. But let me put it another way. My father's father, who lived until I was twelve years old, was born in March of 1864, more than a year before the Civil War ended and while the countryside was still overrun by marauding bands of soldiers such as that led by Bart Jenkins. When my father was born the war had been over only thirty-five years. When I was born it had been over for not quite seventy years. In my part of the country during my childhood there was still a sizable population of the children of slave owners and the children of slaves. The knowledge that I have of my family's involvement in slavery I have literally at second hand; I am separated from it by only one generation.

And so when I was a child my inherited language, so protective of a crucial silence at its heart, was still very near to the spiritual crises of its origin. Two decades would pass between my birth and the antisegregation decision of the Supreme Court in 1954. The racist language, which is to say also the racist mentality, was still intact around its silence. I remember being told that Jesus loved the little black boys and girls as well as the little white ones. I even remember a Baptist Sunday school leaflet showing a little black boy in a group of white children standing before the Savior, being suffered to come unto Him. But I remember no attempt to reconcile this alleged divine love of black children with the white people's notion that they were inferior. I suppose it was assumed that if Jesus loved them there was no need for white folks to trouble themselves.

But though the black population in that part of the country was beginning to move northward, largely into the cities of Ohio—under the influence of the old fairy tale that Negroes were welcome and well-liked north of the Ohio—there was still a large black population in Henry County throughout my childhood. They cooked and did housekeeping in most of the houses and worked as fieldhands on most of the farms that I visited as a child. And so the lives and personalities of black people figured large in my experience. But not only that. Given the association, and given the innocence and candor of childhood, it was inevitable that we should come to like and even to love some of those black people. In that way the silence I have spoken of came to be invested with a tension, an anxiety, by which it would either be made impregnable, which is what usually happened, or finally broken.

· 4 ·

When I was three years old Nick Watkins, a black man, came to work for my Grandfather Berry. I don't remember when he came, which is to say that I don't remember not knowing him. When I was older and Nick and I would reminisce about the beginnings of our friendship, he used to laugh and tell me that when he first came I would follow him around calling him Tommy. Tommy was the hand who had lived there just before Nick. It was one of those conversations that are repeated ritually between friends. I would ask Nick to tell how it had been when he first came, and he would always tell about me calling him Tommy, and he would laugh. When I was eight or nine the story was important to me because it meant that Nick and I had known each other since way back, and were old buddies.

I have no idea of Nick's age when I first knew him. He must have been in his late fifties, and he worked for us until his death in, I believe, 1945—a period of about eight years. During that time one of my two or three chief ambitions was to be with him. With my brother or by myself, I dogged his steps. So faithful a follower, and so young and self-important and venturesome as I was, I must have been a trial to him. But he never ran out of patience.

From something philosophical and serene in that patience, and from a few things he said to me, I know that Nick had worked hard ever since his childhood. He told me that when he was a small boy he had worked for a harsh white woman, a widow or a spinster. When he milked, the cow would often kick the bucket over, and he would have to carry it back to the house empty, and the white woman would whip him. He had worked for hard bosses. Like thousands of others of his race he had lived from childhood with the knowledge that his fate was to do the hardest of work for the smallest of wages, and that there was no hope of living any other way.

White people thought of Nick as "a good nigger," and within the terms of that designation he had lived his life. But in my memory of him, and I think in fact, he was possessed of a considerable dignity. I think this was because there was a very conscious peace and faithfulness that he had made between himself and his lot. When there was work to be done, he did it dependably and steadily and well, and thus escaped the indignity of being bossed. I do not remember seeing him servile or obsequious. My grandfather, within the bounds of the racial bias, thought highly of him. He admired him particularly, I remember, as a teamster, and was always pointing him out to me as an example: "Look a yonder how old Nick sets up to drive his mules. Look how he takes hold of the lines. Remember that, and you'll know something."

In the eight or so years that Nick lived on the place, he and my grandfather spent hundreds and hundreds of work days together. When Nick first came there my grandfather was already in his seventies. Beyond puttering around and "seeing to things," which he did compulsively as long as he could stand up, he had come to the end of his working time. But despite the fact that my father had quietly begun to make many of the decisions in the running of the farm, and had assumed perhaps most of the real worries of running it, the old man still thought of himself as the sovereign ruler there, and it could be a costly mistake to attempt to deal with him on the assumption that he was not. He still got up at four o'clock as he always had, and when Nick and the other men on the place went to work he would be with them, on horseback, following the mule teams to the field. He rode a big bay mare named Rose; he would continue to ride her past the time when he could get into the saddle by himself. Through the long summer days he would stay with Nick, sitting and watching and talking, reminiscing, or riding behind him as he drove the rounds of a pasture on a mowing machine. When there was work that he could do, he would be into it until he tired out, and then he would invent an errand so he could get away with dignity.

Given Nick's steadiness at work, I don't think my grandfather stayed with him to boss him. I think he stayed so close because he couldn't stand not to be near what was going on, and because he needed the company of men of his own kind, working men. I have the clearest memory of the two of them passing again and again in the slowly shortening rounds of a big pasture, Nick driving a team of good black mules hitched to a mowing machine, my grandfather on the mare always only two or three steps behind the cutter bar. I don't know where I am in the memory, perhaps watching from the shade of some bush in a fencerow. In the bright hot sun of the summer day they pass out of sight and the whole landscape falls quiet. And then I hear the chuckling of the machine again, and then I see the mules' ears and my grandfather's hat appear over the top of the ridge, and they all come back into sight and pass around again. Within the steady monotonous racket of the machine, they keep a long silence, rich, it seems to me, with the deep camaraderie of men who have known hard work all their lives. Though their long labor in barns and fields had been spent in radically different states of mind, with radically different expectations, it was a common ground and a bond between them—never by men of their different colors, in that time and place, to be openly acknowledged or spoken of. Nick drives on and on into the day, deep in his silence, erect, alert and solemn faced with the patience that has kept with him through thousands of such days before, the elemental reassurance that dinnertime will come, and then quitting time, supper and rest. Behind him as the day lengthens, my grandfather dozes on the mare; when he sways in the saddle the mare steps under him, keeping him upright. Nick would claim that the mare did this out of a conscious sense of responsibility, and maybe she did.

On those days I know that Nick lived in constant fear that the mare too would doze and step over the cutter bar, and would be cut and would throw her rider before the mules could be stopped. Despite my grandfather's unshakable devotion to the idea that he was still in charge of things, it was clearly Nick who bore the great responsibility of those days. Because of childishness or whatever, the old man absolutely refused to accept the limits of age. He was fiercely headstrong in everything, and so was constantly on the verge of doing some damage to himself. I can see Nick working along, pretending not to watch him, but watching him all the same out of the corner of his eye, and then hustling anxiously to the rescue: "Whoa, boss. Whoa. Wait, boss." When he had my brother and me, and maybe another boy or two, to look after as well, Nick must have been driven well nigh out of his mind, but he never showed it.

When they were in the mowing or other such work, Nick and my grandfather were hard to associate with. Of course we could get on horseback ourselves and ride along behind the old man's mare, but it was impossible to talk and was consequently boring. But there was other work, such as fencing or the handwork in the crops, that allowed the possibility of conversation, and whenever we could we got into that—in everybody's way, whether we played or tried to help, often getting scolded, often aware when we were not being scolded that we were being stoically put up with, but occasionally getting the delicious sense that we were being kindly indulged and catered to for all our sakes, or more rarely that we were being of use.

I remember one fine day we spent with Nick and our grandfather, cutting a young sassafras thicket that had grown up on the back of the place. Nick would fell the little trees with his ax, cutting them off about waist high, so that when they sprouted the cattle would browse off the foliage and so finally kill them. We would pile the trees high on the sled, my brother and I would lie on the mass of springy branches, in the spiced sweetness of that foliage, among the pretty leaves and berries, and Nick would drive us down the hill to unload the sled in a wash that our grandfather was trying to heal.

That was quiet slow work, good for talk. At such times the four of us would often go through a conversation about taking care of Nick when he got old. I don't remember how this conversation would start. Perhaps Nick would bring the subject up out of some anxiety he had about it. But our grandfather would say, "Don't you worry, Nick. These boys'll take care of you."

And one of us would say, "Yessir, Nick, we sure will."

And our grandfather would shake his head in sober emphasis and say, "By God, they'll do it!"

Usually, then, there would follow an elaborately detailed fantasy in which Nick would live through a long carefree old age, with good foxhounds and time to hunt, looked after by my brother and me who by then would have grown up to be lawyers or farmers.

Another place we used to talk was in the barn. Usually this would be on a rainy day, or in the late evening after work. Nick and the old man would sit in the big doorway on upturned buckets, gazing out into the lot. They would talk about old times. Or we would all talk about horses, and our grandfather would go through his plan to buy six good colts for my brother and me to break and train. Or we would go through the plan for Nick's old age.

Or our grandfather would get into a recurrent plan all his own about buying a machine, which was his word for automobile. According to the plan, he would buy a good new machine, and Nick would drive it, and they would go to town and to "Louis-ville" and maybe other places. The intriguing thing about this plan was that it was based on the old man's reasoning that since Nick was a fine teamster he was therefore a fine automobile driver. Which Nick wasn't; he couldn't drive an automobile at all. But as long as Nick lived, our grandfather clung to that dream of buying a good machine. Under the spell of his own talk about it, he always believed that he was right on the verge of doing it.

We also talked about the war that was being fought "across the waters." The two men were deeply impressed with the magnitude of the war and with the ominous new weapons that were being used in it. I remember sitting there in the barn door one day and hearing our grandfather say to Nick: "They got cannons now that'll shoot clean across the water. Good God Amighty!" I suppose he meant the English Channel, but I thought then that he meant the ocean. It was one of the ways the war and modern times became immediate to my imagination.

A place I especially liked to be with Nick was at the woodpile. At his house and at my grandparents' the cooking was still done on wood ranges, and Nick had to keep both kitchens supplied with stove wood. The poles would be laid up in a sawbuck and sawed to the proper lengths with a crosscut saw, and then the sawed lengths would be split on the chopping block with an ax. It was a daily thing throughout the year, but more wood was needed of course in the winter than in the summer. When I was around I would often help Nick with the sawing, and then sit up on the sawbuck to watch while he did the splitting, and then I would help him carry the wood in to the woodbox in the kitchen. Those times I would carry on long conversations, mostly by myself; Nick, who needed his breath for the work, would reply in grunts and monosyllables.

Summer and winter he wore two pairs of pants, usually an old pair of dress pants with a belt under a pair of bib overalls, swearing they kept him cool in hot weather and warm in cold. Like my grandfather, he often wore an old pair of leather puttees, or he would have his pants legs tied snugly above his shoe tops with a piece of twine. This, he liked to tell us, was to keep the snakes and mice from running up his britches legs. He wore old felt hats that were stained and sweaty and shaped to his character. He had a sober open dignified face and gentle manners, was quick to smile and to laugh. His teeth were ambeer-stained from chewing tobacco. His hands were as hard as leather; one of my hopes was someday to have hands as hard as his. He seemed instinctively to be a capable handler of stock. He could talk untiringly of good saddle horses and good work teams that he had known. He was an incurable fox hunter and was never without a hound or two. I think he found it easy to be solitary and quiet.

I heard my grandfather say to him one day: "Nick, you're the first darkie I ever saw who didn't sing while he worked."

But there were times, I knew, when Nick did sing. It was only one little snatch of a song that he sang. When the two of us would go on horseback to the store or to see about some stock—Nick on my grandfather's mare, I on a pony—and we had finished our errand and started home, Nick would often sing: "Get along home, home, Cindy, get along home!" And he would laugh.

"Sing it again," I would say.

And he would sing it again.

· 5 ·

But before I can tell any more about Nick, I will have to tell about Aunt Georgie. She came to live in the little two-room house with Nick in perhaps the third year he worked for us. Why did we call her Aunt when we never called Nick Uncle? I suppose it was because Nick was informal and she was formal. I remember my grandparents insisting that my brother and I should say Uncle Nick, but we would never do it. Our friendship was somehow too democratic for that. They might as well have insisted that we boys call each other mister. But we used the title Aunt Georgie from the first. She was a woman of a rather stiff dignity and a certain aloofness, and the term of respect was clearly in order.

She was short and squat, bowlegged, bent, her hands crooked with arthritis, her two or three snaggling front teeth stained with snuff. I suppose she was ugly—though I don't believe I ever made that judgment in those days. She looked like Aunt Georgie, who looked like nobody else.

Her arrival at Nick's house suddenly made that one of the most intriguing places that my brother and I had ever known. We began to spend a lot of our time there just sitting and talking. She would always greet us and make us at home with a most gracious display of pleasure in seeing us. Though she could cackle with delight like an old child, though she would periodically interrupt her conversation to spit ambeer into a coffee can she kept beside her chair, there was always a reserve about her, an almost haughty mannerliness that gave a peculiar sense of *occasion* to these visits. When she would invite us to eat supper, as she sometimes did, her manner would impose a curious self-consciousness on us—not a *racial* self-consciousness, but the demanding self-consciousness of a child who has been made, in the fullest sense, the guest of an adult, and of whom therefore a certain dignity is expected. Her house was one of the few places I visited as a child where I am certain I always behaved well. There was something in her presence that kept you always conscious of how you were acting; in response to her you became capable of social delicacy.

Thinking of her now, in spite of my rich experience of her, I realize how little I really *know* about her. The same is true of Nick. I knew them as a child knows people, as they revealed themselves to a child. What they were in themselves, as they spoke to each other, or thought in solitude, I can only surmise from that child's knowledge. I will never know.

Aunt Georgie had lived in a small rural community thirty or forty miles away. She had also lived in Louisville, where I believe she had relatives. She was a great reader of the Bible, and I assume of tracts of various sorts, and I don't know what else. The knowledge that came out in her talk—fantastical, superstitious, occult, theological, Biblical, autobiographical, medical, historical—was amazing in variety and extent. She was one of the most intricate and powerful characters I have ever known. Perhaps not twenty-five percent of her knowledge was subject to any kind of proof—a lot of it was the stuff of unwritten fairy tales and holy books, a lot I think she had made up herself—but all of it, every last occult or imaginary scrap of it, was caught up and held together in the force of her personality. Nothing was odd to her, nothing she knew stood aside from her unassimilated into the restless wayward omnivorous force of her mind. I write of her with fear that I will misrepresent or underestimate her. I believe she had great intelligence, which had been forced to grow and form itself on the strange straggling wildly heterogeneous bits of information that sifted down to her through various leaks in the stratification of white society.

The character of Aunt Fanny in my book *A Place on Earth* is to some extent modeled on Aunt Georgie: "She's an accomplished seamstress, and the room is filled with her work: quilts, crocheted doilies, a linen wall-hanging with the Lord's Prayer embroidered on it in threads of many colors. In the house she's nearly always occupied with her needle, always complaining of her dim eyesight and arthritic hands. Her dark hands, though painfully crooked and drawn by the disease, are still . . . dexterous and capable. She's extremely attentive to them, always anointing them with salves and ointments of her own making. The fingers wear rings made of copper wire, which she believes to have the power of prevention and healing. She's an excellent persistent canny gardener. The garden beside the house is her work. She makes of its small space an amplitude . . . rows of vegetables and flowers—and herbs, for which she knows the recipes and the uses." If that is her daylight aspect, there is also an aspect of darkness: ". . . the intricate quilts which are always prominent in the room, on the bed or the quilting frame . . . always seem threatened, like earthquake country, by an ominous nearness of darkness in the character of their creator. Aunt Fanny has seen the Devil, not once but often, especially in her youth, and she calls him familiarly by his name: Red Sam. Her obsessions are Hell and Africa, and she has the darkest, most fire-lit notions of both. Her idea of Africa is a hair-raising blend of lore and hearsay and imagination. She thinks of it with nostalgia and longing—a kind of earthly Other Shore, Eden and Heaven—and yet she fears it because of its presumed darkness, its endless jungles, its stock of deliberately malevolent serpents and man-eating beasts. And by the thought of Hell she's held as endlessly fascinated as if her dearest ambition is to go there. She can talk at any length about it, cataloguing its tortures and labyrinths in almost loving detail. . . . Stooped in the light of a coal-oil lamp at night, following her finger down some threatening page of the Bible, her glasses opaquely reflecting the yellow of the lamp, her pigtails sticking out like compass points around her head, she looks like a black Witch of Endor.

"She possesses a nearly inexhaustible lore of snakes and deaths, and bottomless caves and pools, and mysteries and ghosts and wonders."

But the purpose of Aunt Fanny in that book is not to represent Aunt Georgie, and she comes off as a much simpler character. Aunt Fanny had spent all her life in the country, but Aunt Georgie had lived for some time in the city, and her mind, in its way of rambling and sampling, had become curiously cosmopolitan. Like Aunt Fanny, she had an obsession with Africa, but I think it must have started with her under the influence of the Back to Africa movement. She must at some time or other have heard speakers involved in this movement, for I remember her quoting someone who said, "Don't let them tell you they won't know you when you go back. They know their own people, and they'll *welcome* you." There was much more of this talk, but I had no context in which to place it and understand it, and so I have lost the memory. She used to tell a lot of stories about Africa, and I remember only one of them: a story of a woman and her small child who somehow happened to be passing through the jungle alone. A lion was following them, and the woman was terrified. They ran on until they were exhausted and could go no farther. Not knowing what else to do, the woman resigned herself and sat down to wait for death. And the lion came up to them. But instead of attacking, he walked calmly up and laid his paw in the woman's lap. She saw that the paw had a thorn in it that had made a very sore wound. She removed the thorn and treated the wound, and the lion became her protector, driving away the other large animals that threatened them in the jungle, hunting and providing for them, and in all ways taking care of them. I suppose I remember that story among all the others she told because I visualized it very clearly as she told it; it has stayed in my mind all these years with the straightforwardness and innocence of a Rousseau painting, but darker, the foliage ranker and more blurred in detail. But also I have remembered it, I think, because of the sense that began then, and that remains poignant in the memory, that the lion had become the woman's husband.

It was from Aunt Georgie, sitting and listening to her by the hour when I was seven and eight and nine and ten years old, that I first heard talk of the question of civil rights for Negroes. Again, I could supply no context for what I heard, and so have forgotten most of it. But one phrase has stuck in my mind along with her manner of saying it. She said that many times the white people had promised the Negro people "a right to the flag," and they never had given it to them. The old woman was capable of a moving eloquence, and I was deeply disturbed by what she said. I remember that, and I remember the indignation of my white elders when I would try to check the point with them. After Aunt Georgie moved away it was probably ten years before I paid attention to any more talk about civil rights, and it was longer than that before I felt again anything like the same disturbed sense of personal responsibility that she made me feel.

She used to tell a story about the end of the First World War, of people dancing wildly through the streets, carrying the Kaiser's head impaled on the end of a fence rail. I keep a clear image of that scene, too. Was it some celebration she had seen in Louisville, at which the Kaiser had been mutilated in effigy? Was it something she had read or imagined? I don't know. I assumed then that it was really the Kaiser's head, that she had seen that barbaric celebration herself, and that it was one of the central events of the history of the world.

Germany was also a sort of obsession with her, I suppose because of the two world wars, and she had nothing good to say for it. If to her Africa was a darkish jungly place of marvels that enticed the deepest roots of her imagination, Germany was a medieval torture chamber, a place of dire purposes and devices, pieces of diabolical machinery. In her sense of it the guillotine had come to be its emblem. It was a sort of earthly hell where people were sent to be punished for such crimes as public drunkenness. According to her, if you were caught drunk once you were *warned*, if you were caught twice you were put in jail, but the *third* time you were put on the train and sent to Germany where the Kaiser would cut your head off. She told of a man and his son in the town of Finchville, Kentucky, who had been caught drunk for the third time. The people of the town went down to the railroad station to witness their condemned neighbors' departure for Germany. Through the coach windows the doomed father and son could be seen finding an empty seat and sitting down together to begin their awesome journey. Over the condemned men and over the watching crowd there hung a great heaviness of finality and fate and horror. She told it as one who had been there and had seen it. And I remember it as if *I* had seen it; it is as vivid in my mind as anything that ever happened to *me*. The first time I heard her tell that story I believe I must have spent an hour or two cross-examining her, trying to find some small mitigation of the implacable finality of it, and she would not yield me the tiniest possibility of hope. Thinking about it now I feel the same contraction of despair that I felt then.

She told about awful sicknesses, and acts of violence, and terrible deaths. There was once a lion tamer who used to put his head in a lion's mouth, and one morning he nicked himself shaving and when he put his head into the lion's mouth that day, the lion tasted his blood and bit his head off. She talked about burials, bodies lying in the ground, dug-up bodies, ghosts.

And snakes. She believed that woman should bruise the head of the serpent with her heel. She would snick them up into little pieces with her sharp hoe. But they fascinated her, too, and they lived in her mind with the incandescence that her imagination gave to everything it touched. She was full of the lore of snakes—little and big snakes, deadly poisonous snakes, infernal snakes, *blue* snakes, snakes with yellow stripes and bright red heads, snakes that sucked cows, snakes that swallowed large animals such as people, hoop snakes. Once there was a woman who was walking in the woods, and her feet got tired and she sat down on a log to rest, and she took off her shoe and beat it on the log to dislodge a rock that was in it, and slowly that log began to *move*. My goodness gracious sakes alive!

The most formidable snake of all was the hoop snake. The hoop snake traveled by the law of gravity—a concept as staggering to the mind as atomic energy or perpetual motion. The hoop snake could travel on his belly like any other snake, but when he found himself on the top of a hill he was apt to whip himself up into the shape of a wheel, and go flying off down the slope at a dazzling speed. Once he had started his descent, of course, he had no sense of direction, and no way to stop or to turn aside and he had a deadly poisonous sharp point on the end of his tail that killed whatever it touched. Trees, horses and cattle, cats, dogs, men, women, and even *boys* were all brought down, like grass before the breath of the Lord, in the furious free-wheeling descent of the hoop snake, quicker than the eye. How could you know when he was coming? You couldn't. How could you get out of his way? You couldn't.

It has occurred to me to wonder if there wasn't a degree of conscious delight that Aunt Georgie took in scaring the wits out of two gullible little white boys. I expect there was. There was undoubtedly some impulse of racial vengeance in it; and it was bound to have given her a sense of power. But there was no cynicism in it; she believed what she said. I think, in fact, that she was motivated somewhat by a spirit of evangelism; she was instructing us, warning us against human evils, alerting us to the presence of ominous powers. Also she must have been lonely; we were company for her, and these things that she had on her mind were what she naturally talked to us about. And probably beyond any other reasons was that, like all naturally talkative people, she loved to listen to herself and to provide herself with occasions for eloquence.

But she was also a tireless loving gardener, a rambler in the fields, a gatherer of herbs and mushrooms, a raiser of chickens. And she talked well about all these things. She was a marvelous teller of what went on around the farm: How the mules ran the goat and the goat jumped up in the loading chute, safe, and looked back at the mules and wagged his head as if to say, "Uh *huh*!" How the hawk got after her chickens, and how she got her old self out of the house just in time and said, "Whoooeee! Hi! Get *out* of here, you *devil* you, and don't you come *back!*"

She knew about healing herbs and tonics and poultices and ointments. In those years I was always worrying about being skinny. I knew from the comic books that a ninety-eight-pound weakling was one of the worst things you could grow up to be; I foresaw my fate, and dreaded it. I confided my worry to Aunt Georgie, as I did to nearly everybody who seemed willing to listen, and she instantly prescribed a concoction known as Dr. Bell's Pine Tar Honey. By propounding the cure she ratified the ill; no one would ever persuade me again that I was not disastrously skinny. But Dr. Bell's Pine Tar Honey was nowhere to be found. No drugstore had it. The more I failed to find it, the more I believed in its power. It could turn a skinny boy into a *normal* boy. It was the elusive philosopher's stone of my childhood. And Aunt Georgie stood by her truth. She never quit recommending it. She would recommend no substitute.

She and Nick never married, though I believe she never abandoned the hope that they would. She always referred to Nick, flirtatiously and a little wistfully, as Nickum-Nackum. But Nick, with what I believe to have been a very pointed discretion, always called her *Miss* Georgie.

· 6 ·

If Aunt Georgie was formal and austere, Nick was casual and familiar. If the bent of her mind was often otherworldly, Nick's belonged incorrigibly to this world; he was a man of the fields and the barns and the long nighttime courses of fox hunts. When he spoke of the Lord he called him, as my grandfather did, the Old Marster, by which they meant a god of mystery, the maker of weather and seasons, of abundance and dearth, of growth and death—a god far more remote, and far less talkative, than the god of the churches.

At night after I had finished supper in my grandmother's kitchen I would often walk down across the field to where Nick's house sat at the corner of the woods. He would come out, lighting his pipe, and we would sit down on the stones of the doorstep, and Nick would smoke and we would talk while it got dark and the stars came out. Up the hill we could see the lighted windows of my grandparents' house. In front of us the sloping pasture joined the woods. The woods would become deep and softly massive in its darkness. At dusk a toad who lived under the doorstep would come out, and always we would notice him and Nick would comment that he lived there and that he came out every night. Often as we sat there, comfortable with all the outdoors and the night before us, Aunt Georgie would be sitting by the lamp in the house behind us, reading aloud from the Bible, or trying to lecture to Nick on the imminence of eternity, urging him to think of the salvation of his soul. Nick's reluctance to get disturbed over such matters was always a worry to her. Occasionally she would call out the door: "Nickum-Nackum? Are you listening to me?" and Nick would serenely interrupt whatever he was telling me—"Yessum, Miss Georgie"—and go on as before.

What we would often be talking about was a fine foxhound named Waxy that Nick had owned a long time ago. He would tell of the old fox hunts, saying who the hunters had been and what kind of dogs they'd had. He would tell over the whole course of some hunt. By the time the race was over his Waxy would always have far outdistanced all the other dogs, and everybody would have exclaimed over what a great, fleet, wise hound she was, and perhaps somebody would have tried to buy her from Nick at a high price, which Nick would never take. Thinking about it since, I have had the feeling that those dogs so far outhunted and outrun by Nick's Waxy were white men's dogs. But I don't know for sure. In addition to telling how well Waxy had performed in some fox race or other, Nick would always tell how she looked, how she was marked and made. And he would frequently comment that Waxy was a fine name for a foxhound. He had thought a lot about how things ought to be named. In his mind he had lists of the best names for milk cows and horses and dogs. Blanche, I remember, he thought to be the prettiest name for a certain kind of light-coated Jersey cow. As long as he was with us I don't think he ever had the luck to give that name to a cow. Among others whose names I have forgotten, I remember that he milked one he called Mrs. Williams.

There were certain worldly ideals that always accompanied him, as hauntingly, I think, as Aunt Georgie was accompanied by devils and angels and snakes and ghosts. There was the ideal foxhound and the ideal team of mules and the ideal saddle horse, and he could always name some animal he had known that had not been quite perfect but had come close. Someday he would like to own a fox-hound like Waxy but just a little better. Someday he would like to work a team of gray mare mules each just a little better than the one named Fanny that my grandfather owned.

We talked a great deal about the ideal saddle horse, because I per-sistently believed that I was going to pick out and buy one of my own. In the absence of any particular horse that I intended to buy, the conversational possibilities of this subject were nearly without limit. Listing points of color, conformation, breeding, disposition, size, and gait, we would arrive within a glimpse of the elusive out-lines of the ideal. And then, supposing some divergence from one of the characteristics we had named, we might prefigure a horse of an-other kind. We were like those experts who from a track or a single bone can reconstruct an extinct animal: give us a color or a trait of conformation or character, and we could produce a horse to go with it. And once we had the horse, we had to settle on a name and on the way it should be broke and fed and kept.

But our *great* plan, the epic of our conversation, was to go camp-ing and hunting in the mountains. I don't think that either Nick or my brother and I knew very much about the mountains. None of us had been there. My own idea seems to have blended what I had read of the virgin Kentucky woods of Boone's time with Aunt Georgie's version of Africa. My brother and I believed there was a great tract of wilderness in the mountains, thickly populated with deer and bears and black panthers and mountain lions. We thought we would go up there and kill some of those beasts and eat their flesh and dress in their skins and make ornaments and weapons out of their long teeth, and live in the untouched maidenhood of history.

I don't know what idea Nick may have had of the mountains; he always seemed more or less to go along with our idea of them; whether or not he contributed to the notions we had, I don't remember. Though he was an ignorant man, he was knowing and skilled in the realities that had been available to him, and so he was bound to have known that we would never make any such trip. But he elaborated this plan with us year after year; it was, in fact, in many ways more his creature than ours. It was generous—one of the most generous things anybody ever did for us. And yet it was more than generous, for I think Nick believed in that trip as a novelist believes in his novel: his imagination was touched by it; he couldn't resist it.

We were going to get new red tassels to hang on the mules' harness, and polish the brass knobs on their hames. And then one night we were going to load the wagon—we had told over many times what all we were going to put in it. And the next morning early, way before daylight so my grandfather wouldn't catch us, we would slip off and go to the mountains. We had a highly evolved sense of the grandeur of the spectacle we would make as we went through New Castle, where everybody who saw us would know where we were going and what a fine adventure it was. Here we would come through the town just as everybody was getting up and out into the street. Nick would be driving, my brother and I sitting on either side of him, his ready henchmen. We would have the mules in a spanking trot, the harness jangling, the red tassels swinging, and everything fine—right on through town past the last house. From there to the tall wilderness where we would make our camp we had no plans. The trip didn't interest us after people we knew quit watching.

When we got to the mountains we were going to build a log cabin, and we talked a lot about the proper design and construction of that. And there were any number of other matters, such as cooking, and sewing the clothes we would make out of the skins of animals. Sometimes, talking of the more domestic aspects of our trip, we would get into a bind and have to plan to take Aunt Georgie. She never could work up much enthusiasm for the project; it was too mundane for her.

There were several times when we actually named the day of our departure, and my brother and I went to bed expecting to leave in the morning. We had agreed that to wake us up Nick would rattle a few tin cans in the milk bucket. But we never woke up until too late. I remember going out one morning and finding the very tin cans that Nick had rattled floating in the rain barrel. Later I realized that of course Nick had never rattled those cans or any others. But in the years since I have often imagined him taking the time to put those cans there for me to see, and then slipping off to his day's work—conspiring with himself like Santa Claus to deceive and please me.

In the present time, when the working man in the old sense of the phrase is so rapidly disappearing from the scene, his conversation smothered in the noise of machinery, it may be necessary to point out that such talk as we carried on with Nick was by no means uncommon among the farming people of that place, and I assume of other places as well. It was one of the natural products and pleasures of the life there. With the hands occupied in the work, the mind was set free; and since there was often considerable misery in the work, the mind turned naturally to what would be desirable or pleasant. When one was at work with people with whom one had worked

many days or years before, one naturally spoke of the good things
that were on one's mind. And once the conversation was started, it
began to be a source of pleasure in itself, producing and requiring
an energy that propelled it beyond the bounds of reality or practicality. As long as one was talking about what would be good, why
not go ahead and talk about what would be *really* good? My childhood was surrounded by a communal daydreaming, the richest
sort of imaginative talk, that began in this way—in work, in the
misery of work, to make the work bearable and even pleasant. Such
talk ranged all the way from a kind of sensuous realism to utter fantasy, but because the bounds of possibility were almost always ignored I would say that the impetus was always that of fantasy. I have
heard crews of men, weary and hungry and hot near the end of a
day's work, construct long elaborate conversations on the subject
of what would be good to eat and drink, dwelling at length and with
subtlety on the taste and the hotness or the coldness of various
dishes and beverages, and on combinations of dishes and beverages, the menu lengthening far beyond the capacity of any living
stomach. I knew one man who every year got himself through the
ordeal of the tobacco harvest by elaborating from one day to the
next the fantasy of an epical picnic and celebration which was always to occur as soon as the work was done—and which never did
occur except, richly, marvelously, in the minds of his listeners. Such
talk could be about anything: where you would like to go, what you
would like to do when you got there, what you would like to be able
to buy, what would be a good kind of a farm, what science was
likely to do, and so on.

Nick often had fox hunting on his mind, and he always knew
where there was a fox, and he was always going to hunt as soon as
he had time. Occasionally he *would* have time—a wet afternoon or
a night when he didn't feel too tired—and he would go, and would

sometimes take one of us. I like the thought of Nick, alone as he often was, out in the woods and the fields at night with his dogs. I think he transcended his lot then, and was free in the countryside and in himself—beyond anybody's knowledge of where he was and anybody's notion of what he ought to do and anybody's claim on his time, his dogs mouthing out there in the dark, and all his senses with them, discovering the way the fox had gone. I don't remember much about any hunt I ever made with him, but I do remember the sense of accompanying him outside the boundaries of his life as a servant, into that part of his life that clearly belonged to him, in which he was competent and knowing. And I remember how it felt to be riding sleepily along on the pony late at night, the country all dark around us, not talking, not sure where we were going. Nick would be ahead of me on old Rose, and I could hear her footsteps soft on the grass, or hard on the rocks when we crossed a creek. I knew that Nick knew where we were, and I felt comfortable and familiar with the dark because of that.

When Joe Louis fought we would eat supper and then walk across the fields to the house of the man who was raising my grandfather's tobacco; we would have been planning for days to go there to hear the fight on the radio. My grandparents had a radio, too, but Nick would never have thought of going there. That he felt comfortable in going to another household of white people and sitting down by the radio with them was always a little embarrassing to me, and it made me a little jealous. And yet I understood it, and never questioned it. It was one of those complex operations of race consciousness that a small child will comprehend with his feelings, and yet perhaps never live long enough to unravel with his mind. The prowess of Joe Louis, anyhow, was something Nick liked to talk about; it obviously meant a great deal to him. And so the championship matches of those days were occasions when I felt called on to manifest my allegiance to Nick. Though I could have listened to the fight in my grandparents' living room, I would go with Nick, and the more my grandmother declared she didn't know why I had to do that the more fierce and clear my loyalty to Nick became.

The people of that house had a boy a little older than I was, and so I also had my own reasons for going there. We boys would listen to the fight and then, while the grownups talked, go out to play, or climb the sugar pear trees and sit up in the branches, eating. And then holding Nick's hand, I would walk with him back home across the dark fields.

One winter there suddenly appeared in the neighborhood a gaunt possessed-looking white man who was, as people said, "crazy on religion" or "religious crazy." He was, I believe, working on a nearby farm. Somehow he discovered Aunt Georgie, and found that she could quote the Bible and talk religion as long as he could. He called Nick Mix, and so in derision and reprisal Nick and my brother and I called *him* Mix, and that was the only name we ever knew him by. We would see him coming over the hill, his ragged clothes flapping in the cold wind, and see him go into the little house. And then after a while we would go down, too, and listen. The tone of their conversations was very pious and oratorical; they more or less preached to each other, and the sessions would go on for hours.

Of it all, I remember only a little fragment: Mix, sitting in a chair facing Aunt Georgie, sticks his right hand out into the air between them, dramatically, and asks her to put hers out there beside it. She does, and then he raises his left hand like a Roman orator and, glaring into her eyes, says: "There they are, Auntie! *There* they are! Look at 'em! One of 'em's white, and one of 'em's black! But *inside*, they both white!"

What impresses me now, as I remember those times, is that while

Mix was never anything but crazy and absurd, ranting mad, Aunt Georgie always seemed perfectly dignified and sane. It seems to me that this testifies very convincingly to the strength of her intelligence: she had *comprehended* the outlandishness of her own mind, and so she could keep a sort of grace before the unbridled extravagance of his. In her way she had faced the worst. The raging of Lear himself would not have perturbed her; she would have told him stories worse than his, and referred him to the appropriate Scripture. To Nick, who took a very detached and secular view of most things, these sessions were a source of ironic amusement. He liked to look over at us through the thick of the uproar and wink.

· 7 ·

I suppose that it is usually the aim of a writer to produce a definitive statement, one that will prove him to be the final authority on what he has said. But though my aim here is to tell the truth as nearly as I am able, I am aware that the truth I am telling may be a very personal one, the truth, that is, as distorted and qualified by my own heritage and personality. I am, after all, writing about people of another race and a radically different heritage, whom I knew only as a child, and whose lives parted from mine nearly a quarter of a century ago. As I write I can hardly help but think of the possibility that if Nick and Aunt Georgie were alive to read this, they might not recognize themselves. And in the face of the extreme racial sensitivity of the present time, I can hardly ignore the possibility that my black contemporaries may find some of my assumptions highly objectionable. And so I write with the feeling that the truth I may tell will not be definitive or objective or even demonstrable, but in the strictest sense subjective, relative to the peculiar self-consciousness of a diseased man struggling toward a cure. I am trying to establish the outlines of an understanding of myself in regard to what was fated to be the continuing crisis of my life, the crisis of racial awareness—

the sense of being doomed by my history to be, if not always a racist, then a man always limited by the inheritance of racism, condemned to be always conscious of the necessity *not* to be a racist, to be always dealing deliberately with the reflexes of racism that are embedded in my mind as deeply at least as the language I speak.

(In the Western tradition of individualism there is the assumption that art can grow out of a personal or a cultural disease, and triumph over it. I no longer believe that. It is related to the idea that a man can achieve personal immortality in a work of art, which I also no longer believe. Though I believe that the liveliest art is suffused with the energy of the creation, and in that sense participates in immortality, I do not believe that any one work of art is immortal any more than I believe that a grove of trees or a nation is immortal. A man cannot be immortal except by saving his soul, and he cannot save his soul except by freeing his body and mind from the destructive forces in his history. A work of art that grows out of a diseased culture has not only the limits of art but the limits of the disease—if it is not an affirmation of the disease, it is a reaction against it. The art of a man divided within himself and against his neighbors, no matter how sophisticated its techniques or how beautiful its forms and textures, will never have the communal *power* of the simplest tribal song.)

There is an inescapable tentativeness in writing of one's own formative experiences: as long as the memory of them stays alive they *remain* formative; the power of growth and change remains in them, and they never become quite predictable in their influence. If memory is in a way the ancestor of consciousness, it yet remains dynamic within consciousness. And so, though I can write about Nick and Aunt Georgie as two of the significant ancestors of my mind, I must also deal with their memory as a live resource, a *power* that will live and change in me as long as I live. To fictionalize them, as I did Aunt Georgie to some extent in *A Place on Earth*, would be to give them an imaginative stability at the cost of oversimplifying them. To attempt to tell the "truth" about them as they really were is to resign oneself to enacting a small fragment of an endless process. Their truth is inexhaustible both in their lives as they were, and in my life as I think they were.

The peculiar power of my memory of them comes, I think, from the fact that all my association with them occurred within a tension between the candor and openness of a child's view of things, and the racial contrivances of the society we lived in. As I have already suggested, there were times when I was inescapably aware of the conflict between what I felt about them, in response to what I knew of them, and the feelings that were prescribed to me by the society's general prejudice against their race. Being with them, it was hard to escape for very long from the sense of racial difference prepared both in their minds and in my own.

The word *nigger* might be thought of as rattling around, with devastating noise and impact, within the silence, that black-man-shaped hollow, inside our language. When the word was spoken abstractly, I believe that it seemed as innocuous and casual to me as any other word. I used it that way myself, in the *absence* of black people, without any consciousness that I was participating in a judgment and a condemnation; certainly I used it without any feeling that my use of it manifested anything that was wrong with *me*. But when it was used with particular reference to a person one cared for, as a child cares, it took on a tremendous force; its power reached ominously over one's sense of things. I remember the shock and confusion I felt one night when, saying good-bye to Nick, I impulsively kissed his hand, which I had held as we brought the milk to the house, and then came into the kitchen to hear: "Lord, child, how can you kiss that old nigger's hand?"

And I remember sitting down at Nick's house one day when he and Aunt Georgie had company. There was a little boy, four or five years old, who was rambunctious and continually on the verge of mischief. To keep him in hand Nick would lean over and rattle his old leather leggings that he had taken off and put behind the drum stove, and he would say to the boy: "John's going to get you. If you don't quit that, John's going to get you." All this—the rattling of the leggings, the threat, the emphatic result—impressed me a good deal, and I wondered about it. Was this John-the-Leggings somebody Nick had thought up on the spur of the moment? Was he one of the many associates of Red Sam? And then it hit me. That John that my friend Nick was speaking of in so formidable a tone was my father! The force of a realization like that is hardly to be measured; it's the sort of thing that can initiate a whole epoch of the development of a mind, and yet remain on as a force. It gave me the strongest sort of a hint of the existence of something large and implacable and rigid that I had been born into, and lived in—something I have been trying to get out of ever since. In justice to my father, I must say that I don't believe his name was used in this way because of anything he had *done*, but because of his place in the system. In spite of my grandfather's insistences to the contrary, Nick knew as I did that my father had become the man really in charge of things. Thus he had entered the formidable role of "boss man": whoever he was, whatever he did, he had the power and the austerity of that role; the society assigned it to him, as it assigned to Nick the role of "nigger."

At times in my childhood I was made to feel the estranging power of this role myself—though I believe always by white men. When I would be playing where the men were working in the fields—I suppose in response to some lapse of tact on my part, some unconscious display of self-importance or arrogance—one of them would sing or quote:

> He ain't the boss, he's the boss's son,
> But he'll be the boss when the boss is done.

A complementary rhyme, which might have been made up as a companion to that, goes this way:

> A naught's a naught and a figger's a figger.
> All for the white man, none for the nigger.

Between them these two little rhymes make a surprisingly complete definition of the values and the class structure of the place and the time of my childhood, and they define its most erosive psychic tensions.

That sense of difference, given the candor and the affection and the high spirits of children, could only beget in us its opposite: a very strong and fierce sense of allegiance. Whenever there was a conflict of interest between Nick and Aunt Georgie and our family, neither my brother nor I ever hesitated to take the side of Nick and Aunt Georgie. We had an uncle who would make a game of insulting Nick in our presence because it tickled him the way we would come to the rescue; we would attack him and fight him as readily as if he had been another child. And there were winter Saturdays that we spent with our goat hitched to a little sled we had made, hauling coal from our grandfather's pile down to Nick's. That was stealing, and we knew it; it had the moral flair and the dangerous loyalty of the adventures of Robin Hood.

But the clearest of all my own acts of taking sides happened at a birthday party my grandmother gave for me when I must have been nine or ten years old. As I remember, she invited all the family and perhaps some of the neighbors. I issued one invitation of my own, to Nick. I believe that in my eagerness to have him come, and assuming that as my friend he ought to be there, I foresaw none of the social awkwardness that I created. But I had, in fact, surrounded us all with the worst sort of discomfort. Nick, trying to compromise between his wish to be kind to me and his embarrassment at my social misconception, quit work at the time of the party and came and sat on the cellar wall behind the house. By that time even I had begun to sense the uneasiness I had created: I had done a thing more powerful than I could have imagined at the time; I had scratched the wound of racism, and all of us, our heads beclouded in the social dream that all was well, were feeling the pain. It was suddenly evident to me that Nick neither would nor could come into the house and be a member of the party. My grandmother, to her credit, allowed me to follow my instincts in dealing with the situation, and I did. I went out and spent the time of the party sitting on the cellar wall with Nick.

It was obviously the only decent thing I could have done; if I had thought of it in moral terms I would have had to see it as my duty. But I didn't. I didn't think of it in moral terms at all. I did simply what I *preferred* to do. If Nick had no place at my party, then I would have no place there either; my place would be where he was. The cellar wall became the place of a definitive enactment of our friendship, in which by the grace of a child's honesty and a man's simple-hearted generosity, we transcended our appointed roles. I like the thought of the two of us sitting out there in the sunny afternoon, eating ice cream and cake, with all my family and my presents in there in the house without me. I was full of a sense of loyalty and love that clarified me to myself as nothing ever had before. It was a time I would like to live again.

· 8 ·

One day when we were all sitting in the barn door, resting and talking, my grandfather sat gazing out a while in silence, and then he pointed to a far corner of the lot and said: "When I'm dead, Nick, I want you to bury me there."

And Nick laughed and said, "Boss, you got to go farther away from here than that."

My grandfather's words bore the forlorn longing to remain in the place, in the midst of the work and the stirring, that had interested him all his life. It was also a characteristic piece of contrariness: if he didn't want to go, then by God he *wouldn't*. Nick's rejoinder admitted how tough it would be on everybody to have such a stubborn old boss staying on there forever, and it told a plain truth: there wasn't to be any staying; good as it might be to be there, we were all going to have to leave.

Those words stand in my memory in high relief; strangely powerful then (it was an exchange that we younger ones quoted over and over in other conversations) they have assumed a power in retrospect that is even greater. That whole scene—the two old men, two or three younger ones, two boys, all looking out that big doorway at the world, and beyond the world—seems to me now not to belong to my childhood at all, but to stand like an illuminated capital at the head of the next chapter. It presages a series of deaths and departures and historical changes that would put an end both to my childhood and to the time and the way of life I knew as a child. Within two or three years of my tenth summer both Nick and my grandfather died, and after Nick's death Aunt Georgie moved away. Also the war ended, and our part of the country moved rapidly into the era of mechanized farming. People, especially those who had worked as hired hands in the fields, began to move to the cities, and the machines moved from the cities out into the fields. Soon nearly everybody had a tractor; the few horses and mules still left in the country were being kept only for old time's sake.

It was a school day in the winter and I was at home in New Castle eating breakfast, when my grandmother telephoned from the farm to tell us that Nick had had a stroke. He had eaten breakfast and was starting to go up to the barn when he fell down in the doorway. He had opened the door before he fell and Aunt Georgie was unable to move him, and so he had lain in the cold for some time before help came. Until he died a few days later he never moved or spoke. I wasn't allowed to go to see him, but afterward my grandmother told me how he had been. He lay there on his back, she said, unable to move, looking up at the ceiling. When she would come in he would recognize her; she could tell that by his eyes. And I am left with that image of him: lying there still as death, his life showing only in his eyes. As if I had been there, I am aware of the intelligence and the gentleness and the sorrow of his eyes. He had fallen completely into the silence that had so nearly surrounded him all his life. It was not the silence of death, which men may speak of with words, and so know each other. It was the racial silence in the speech of white men, the wound of their history, formed three hundred years before my birth to stand between him and me, so that when I think of him now, as important as his memory is to me, it must be partly to wonder if I knew him.

One night not long after Nick's death I went with my father down to the little house to see Aunt Georgie. She had a single lamp lighted in the bedroom, and we went in and sat down. For a time, while they talked, I sat there without hearing, saddened and bewildered by the heavy immanence of change I felt in the room and by Nick's absence from it. And then I began to listen to what was being said. Aunt Georgie's voice was without the readiness of laughter I had always known in her. She spoke quietly and deliberately, avoiding betrayal of her grief. My father was talking, I remember, very gently and generously to her, helping her to get her affairs in order, discussing an insurance policy that Nick had, determining what her needs were. And all at once I realized that Aunt Georgie was going to leave. I hadn't expected it; she was deeply involved in my history and my affections; she had been there what seemed to me a long long time. Perhaps because of those conversations we used to have about taking care of Nick when he got old, I had supposed that such permanent arrangements were made as a matter of course. I interrupted and said something to the effect that I thought Aunt Georgie ought to stay, I didn't want her to go. And they turned to me and explained that it was not possible. She had relatives in Louisville; she would go to live with them. Their few words made it clear to me that there were great and demanding realities that I had never considered: realities of allegiance, realities of economics. I waited in silence then until their talk was finished, and we went out into the winter night and walked back up the hill.

I don't know if I saw Aunt Georgie again before she left. That is the last memory I have of her: strangely detached and remote from the house as though she already no longer lived there, an old woman standing in the yellow lamplight among the shadowy furnishings of the room, stooped and slow as if newly aware of the heaviness of her body.

And so it ended.

· *9* ·

The Child is father of the Man;
And I could wish my days to be
Bound each to each by natural piety.

The lines seem to me bungled. Reading them, I cannot be certain what Wordsworth believed he was saying. But subtracting the tentativeness of "could wish" in the middle line and the vagueness of "natural piety" in the third, it seems to me that he had either made, or was on the verge of making, a profound ethical perception. The first line states not only the psychological commonplace that we are apt to become what we have been *prepared* to become, but also that there is a legacy to be carried over intact from childhood to manhood. The following two lines suggest that there is a moral obligation to live in manhood under the tutelage of the legacy of childhood.

I don't think of children as philosophers and prophets, as Wordsworth apparently did. To me, the great power that children possess is candor; they see the world clear eyed, without prejudice; honesty is not immediately conceived by them as an uncomfortable alternative to lying. On the contrary, the tactics of deceit are customarily given a high priority in the training of a child: *"Don't* say that in front of Aunt So-and-so." What we white Americans call manners and social conventions consist very largely of such tactics. A child is, as we say, impressionable, and acts directly on the basis of his experience. If a person is lovable or respectable, a child will love or respect him without first asking his class or his race or his income.

In a racist society, the candor of a child is therefore extremely threatening. That is also true of a puritanical society, as witness St. Paul, the genius of puritanism: "When I was a child, I spake as a child, I understood as a child, I thought as a child: but when I became a man I put away childish things." The crisis of life in both kinds of society is puberty, when the candor of childhood stands to be invested with sexual power, which would make it a threat both to current assumptions or pretentions, and to the survival of the same in future generations. The sexual man, possessed of a childlike clarity, threatens to *propagate* in the society the results of an elemental honesty which would be devastating. The puritan fears that it would bring about an awareness and a celebration of life in this world, the life of the senses, which would break the hold of the priesthood on the consciences and the purse strings of the populace. The racist fears that a child's honesty empowered by sex might turn in real and open affection toward members of the oppressed race, and so destroy the myth of that race's inferiority. This is perhaps why racism and puritanism have meshed so perfectly in the United States.

To both the racist and the puritan, childhood is not a time of life that we grow out of, as the life of the child grows out of the life of the parent or as a plant grows out of the soil, but a time *and a state of consciousness* to be left behind, to cut oneself off from: "when I became a man, I put away childish things." The child may be joyous, the man must be sober and self-denying; the child may be free, the man is to be "responsible"; the child may be candid in his feelings, the man must be polite, restrained, mindful of the demands of convention; the child may be playful, the man must be industrious. I am not necessarily objecting to the manly virtues, but I am objecting that they should be so exclusively assigned to grownups, and that grownups should be so exclusively restricted to them. A man may have all the prescribed adult virtues and, if he lacks the childhood virtues, still be a dunce and a bore and a liar.

Because of our strict division between childhood and adulthood, we have granted to childhood an exemption from the demands and the values of adult society. Under the dispensations of childhood, a child (at least outside the compartmentalized life of the cities) may cross the boundaries of class and race and property with a good deal of freedom, and his reason for crossing these boundaries is his honesty in the face of his experience. He cuts across backyards, he plays and roams wherever his curiosity or affection leads him, he uses his mind for pleasure, he makes friends among his "inferiors" both black and white, and so on. And then, as soon as his childish pleasure begins to bear the imminence of sexual pleasure, he is suddenly asked to think of "who he is," to dissociate himself from the ways and the associations of his childhood, to "put away childish things" and become a man. As has been often enough pointed out, he doesn't under those demands necessarily become a man in any respectable sense of the word; he is altogether likely to become a perfect snot, useless to his fellows, and destructive of his community and his land. In order that his childhood experience of the common humanity of the black and white races may be submerged in the sense of racial difference, thence in the sense of his own racial superiority, he must learn to look on his childhood as a detachable, inferior, and irrelevant period of his life; in short, he makes himself comfortable among the grownups' lies, and so considers himself a man. (Thus we breed men as spare parts, to be fitted as necessary into the military and industrial and political machines.) This is the meaning of Mark Twain's statement that he quit writing about Tom and Huck because they were ready to grow up and become liars.

What I have been leading up to is the idea that the maintenance of a continuity, a vital connection, between childhood vision and adult experience is a part of the obligation of a moral man. And I am certain that even though such an obligation may not enter the moral consciousness, a man's childhood under favorable circumstances may still become an effectively disciplining force in adult thought and behavior.

And so I have not written at such length out of my memory of Nick and Aunt Georgie in order to give a case history or an example of race relations, nor have I done it in order to confess something of the extent of my involvement in a destructive mental condition. I have written about them in order to reexamine and to clarify what I know to be a moral resource, a part of the vital and formative legacy of my childhood. The memory of them has been one of the persistent forces in the growth of my mind. If I have struggled against the racism that I have found in myself, it has been largely because I have remembered my old sense of allegiance to them. That I have gone back to my native place, to live there mindful of its nature and its possibilities, is partly because of certain things I learned from them or that they exemplified to me.

A great deal has been said about what white racism has cost the black race. As concerns the race as a whole, it is within limits a calculable cost, and it is only just that it should be dwelt upon. But it would be extremely difficult—perhaps it would be impossible—to develop a precise or a useful sense of what the cost has been to a given black *individual*. To say that many highly gifted black men and women have been thoughtlessly misused and wasted in all the years of racism in America is to tell an indisputable truth. But to say that a certain black laborer could have been a great doctor or painter in a society without racism is to make only a conjecture; it is to practice the loose and useless sentiment of Gray's "Elegy":

> Perhaps in this neglected spot is laid
> Some heart once pregnant with celestial fire;
> Hands, that the rod of empire might have swayed,
> Or wak'd to extasy the living lyre.

Perhaps indeed! The emotion is inexact and self-indulgent; it can lead to no useful act.

I am a good deal more grieved by what I am afraid will be the racism of the future than I am about that of the past. The past may to some extent be understood, and it is our obligation to do that, but it cannot be corrected. There is, I am sure, such a thing as a sense of guilt about historical wrongs, but I have the strongest doubts about the usefulness of a guilty conscience as a motivation; a man, I think, can be much more dependably motivated by a sense of what would be desirable than by a sense of what has been deplorable. The historical pressures upon race relations in this country tend always to push us toward two complementary dangers: that, to whites, ancestral guilt will seem an adequate motive; that, to blacks, ancestral bondage will seem an adequate distinction.

I think it would be futile, and perhaps condescending as well, for me to remember Nick and Aunt Georgie only to pity them. There are times, I admit, when I am moved by a necessarily vague pondering over what they might have been. But I am, I think rightly, much more moved, much more clarified and instructed, by what they *were*, for what they were was far from inconsiderable.

Among the supporters, both white and black, of the cause of racial justice in America, there has been a regrettable tendency to deal with the black man's past almost exclusively in terms of what I take to be a *political* oversimplification, which has it that from 1619 to the present the black people in America have been miserable. And this is usually accompanied by the implication that by making black people miserable the white people have made themselves happy. Both of these oversimplifications are, of course, false. I have already spoken of the white misery of white racism, and I want to deal with it at still greater length before I am done. For now I will only say that I don't think the whites have dealt with their misery anything like so well as the blacks have, for as I have also indicated earlier the whites developed almost at once the means of disguising their misery and pretending that it did not exist. The blacks, on the other hand, were not the cause of their misery, it was all coming to them from outside themselves, and so from the beginning they have been dealing directly with it. To say and imply that they have been entirely miserable all these years is to do them a grave injustice and to ignore what the inheritors of that past have to teach us. I do not mean to discount the misery; the misery was real and I doubt that it can be exaggerated. But plunged into that misery without any preparation that could have helped them even to imagine it, these people made in themselves an astonishing endurance, a marvelous ability to survive. They have endured and survived the worst, and in the course of their long ordeal they have developed—as most of white society has not—the understanding and the means both of small private pleasures and of communal grief and celebration and joy.

The great benefit in my childhood friendship with Nick and Aunt Georgie, then, was not an experience of sympathy, though that was involved and was essential, but a prolonged intense contact with lives and minds radically unlike my own, and radically unlike any other that I might have known as a white child among white adults. They don't figure in my memory and in my thoughts about them as objects of pity, but rather as friends and teachers, ancestors you could say, the forebears of certain essential strains in my thinking.

· *10* ·

To give a background to this relationship of white child and black man and woman, I will sketch out here as briefly as I can what I take to be the dominant traits of the mainstream white society I knew as a child:

1. There had begun to be an urban impetus and orientation reaching all the way to the farms, the older farmers thinking of the city as the place for their sons, the sons following suit. The rural towns I knew as a child were in a sense gathering points in a countrywide migration toward the cities. Farming was looked down upon as a hard and generally unremunerative life—facts which the white mentality was more prone to flee than to accommodate within an awareness that there were also amenities. The general aim was to go where the money was to be made; the resources of nativeness and of established community were abandoned without a thought.

2. The main social movement being a migration in the direction of money, society was conceived as a pyramid on which the only desirable or honorable or happy position is the top. People not at the top envied those above them, despised those below them, and apologized for themselves.

3. Happiness was conceived as success. The pragmatization of feeling was a fairly explicit social goal. If it won't get you ahead, if you

can't sell it, forget it, cover it up, speak as if it did not exist. Such humanizing emotions as pleasure in small profitless things, joy, wonder, ecstasy were removed as by an operation on the brain. The only people I ever saw dancing publicly in the town where I grew up were black.

4. Reality was defined by the desire for success. If you were reasonable, followed the rules, obeyed your superiors, asked only practical questions, all would be well. Mysteries either did not exist or would soon be "solved by science." What he could not account for, a man tended either to destroy or ignore. Thus he remained secure.

5. As the puritan denied himself joy on earth in order to have joy in heaven, so the seeker after success denied himself all intermediate pleasures. He would forego impractical feelings, small satisfactions, leisure; he would work day and night, not for any satisfaction it gave him, not even as a duty, but to get to the top. When he got to the top he would rest and enjoy life—as if he would know how. Life was simply a fact, not considered. There was no art of living.

6. People had begun to live lives of a purely theoretical reality, daydreams based on the economics of success. It was as if they had risen off the earth into the purely hypothetical air of their ambition and greed. They were rushing around in the clouds, "getting somewhere," while their native ground, the only meaningful destination, if not the only possible one, lay far below them, abandoned and forgotten, colonized by machines.

7. The church saving the souls of pagans of other continents in the gleeful imperialism of self-righteousness, functioned locally as a fashion show, moral painkiller, women's club, soporific. I recall the general panic in a certain central Kentucky Baptist church when two black Africans, converts of the foreign missions program, turned up on the home ground and applied for membership.

8. Knowledge was conceived as a way to get money. This seems to have involved an unconscious wish to streamline the mind, strip it of all knowledge which would not predictably *function*.

9. There were the local aristocracies of old families which once at least had money. In my experience these have consisted mostly of little bands of widows and derelict wives playing bridge, gossiping,

drinking and hiding the bottle, complaining, grieving ostentatiously over each other but really over themselves.

10. We knew and took for granted: marriage without love; sex without joy; drink without conviviality; birth, celebration, and death without adequate ceremony; faith without doubt or trial; belief without deeds; manners without generosity; "good English" without exact speech, without honesty, without literacy.

This was, and is, a society artificial in the extreme, both in its values and in its physical appurtenances and relationships. In comparison to certain "heathen" societies it has seen fit to despise, it is as flimsy and temporary as a daily newspaper. It is ephemeral, shallow, fashion ridden, diseased by the sense of its own transience. It is always feverishly changing its appearances and its affectations, and yet at its heart it has always the same fear, the same boredom asking to be diverted by such changes. It is stifling. Nothing true can be said in its terms. From it one American writer after another has had to detach himself in order to speak.

The commonest form of escape or dissociation is obscenity. Such a society is fanatically against obscenity, because it is so vulnerable to it. Obscenity is nothing more than the voice of those persistent crude and demanding realities which the society has refused to contend with and so has had to ignore with the greatest care. Its voice of moral authority always speaks with the implication that it is a virgin on a lifelong fast. Its voice is very much the voice of Mosgrove in *Kentucky Cavaliers in Dixie*; if unpleasant facts must be dealt with then they are dealt with *elegantly*—on the assumption that they are thus made pleasant. And to those who subscribe to the pretenses of such language they *are* in effect made pleasant. In a situation like that obscene words assume an uncanny power. They are irresistible. Sensing their power, boys take to the use of them often before they start to school. When I met a boy my own age who did not swear and blackguard like a grownup I thought him remarkably spiritless or mentally deficient.

Though as long as the old prudery lasts the obscene vocabulary will continue to possess an unusual and very necessary energy, the device of mentioning the unmentionable seems to me a clumsy, unintelligent, and finally a hopeless way to oppose what is wrong with us. The alternative is to speak out of the sense of another way of life or state of mind that will serve as a measure of our own life, and that might conceivably offer usable alternatives. The interest of such writers as Eliot and Pound in the cultures of other places and times has been made much of, and I believe rightly. But there is another interest, with a considerable tradition in American literature, that has received less attention, and which is at least equally important: that is an interest in the lives of the poor, not insofar as they are poor, but insofar as, being poor, they have made their lives, often with considerable success, outside the social pretenses and economic obsession of the mainstream of the society.

One thinks of Thoreau always examining with the greatest interest the lives, not of Emerson and the other successful men of Concord, but of small farmers, fishermen and trappers, woodcutters—often finding in them an integrity, a competent self-satisfying intelligence, a joy in small things, a consciousness of meaning that would delight and comfort him. When he went to the woods he lived in the rebuilt shanty of a destitute laborer; it was not to romanticize poverty or to sympathize with it, but to find out what it would show him outside the decorous walls of success and respectability—to learn the use of it.

One thinks of Melville and his high interest in the forecastle life of a whaling ship, in the trades of carpentry and blacksmithing. One thinks of Mark Twain, turning back for his truth and sanity to his childhood among the slaves and farmers and river people in Hannibal, Missouri. One thinks of the great weight in the work of Faulkner of his minute attention to the lives and the minds of Mississippi Negroes.

I have in mind two poems I want to quote to illustrate what I am saying. Neither one, I think, attempts to romanticize poverty—the facts remain as they are—but both come of an excited sense of the realness of the reality, the *poor* reality, that lies beyond the tightly focused interests and the staid adornments of the consciously successful. In both there is, as if suddenly, an uprising of the old truth that it can be profoundly liberating to be free of the claims of money. The first is by William Carlos Williams:

The Poor

It's the anarchy of poverty
delights me, the old
yellow wooden house indented
among the new brick tenements

Or a cast iron balcony
with panels showing oak branches
in full leaf. It fits
the dress of the children

reflecting every stage and
custom of necessity—
chimneys, roofs, fences of
wood and metal in an unfenced

age and enclosing next to
nothing at all: the old man
in a sweater and soft black
hat who sweeps the sidewalk—

his own ten feet of it—
in a wind that fitfully
turning his corner has
overwhelmed the entire city

The second is by Ezra Pound:

Salutation

O generation of the thoroughly smug
*   and thoroughly uncomfortable,*
I have seen fishermen picnicking in the sun,
I have seen them with untidy families,
I have seen their smiles full of teeth
*   and heard ungainly laughter.*
And I am happier than you are,
And they were happier than I am;
And the fish swim in the lake
*   and do not even own clothing.*

Having described the working of that social-literary process as I understand it, I would like to go back to the list I made at the beginning of the chapter and qualify it, not by changing it but by adding something to it. I stand by the list, and I believe in the existence of the condition it describes, but I also am aware that its statements function as haltingly and inexactly as any other generalizations. If I were to come upon that list on a page written by another man, my immediate reaction would be to insist that it is too much a generalization, that it describes tendencies in which people are involved only more or less; and I would begin to think of the exceptions to it that I know. And I must do this here, for it was by way of the exceptions that I came to know and to care for Nick and Aunt Georgie in the first place. And perhaps I have had to *become* an exception in order to finally realize as far as I have what my knowledge of them has meant to me.

· *II* ·

Though my father had left the farm and become a lawyer, he practiced in the county seat, New Castle, only about six miles from my grandfather's farm where the last three generations of us had been born. Living always within reach of it, we were always under its influence. From the first I was aware of the insistent claims and pressures of the success-orientation that ruled the lives of the white society. But my father, having been carried those six miles by the impetus of the farm-to-city migration, seems to have felt himself overtaken by the claims of his place of origin and of the old life that he had left. He never went any farther away. And though he had become in a sense more than a farmer, there was also a sense in which he refused to become less. In addition to, and in spite of, all else that he had become, he *remained* a farmer. Alongside the knowledge and abilities by which he functioned in courthouses and offices, there remained an indissoluble devotion to the life of the earth. He kept the farmer's passion that sees beyond the market values into the intricacy and beauty of the lives of things, and that hungers to preserve and enrich the land. To him crops and animals were not only to be sold, but to be studied, understood, admired for their own sakes. He divided his interest, his life, and his mind between his profession and his land. If he had been less willing to endure the considerable effort and strain of this division, if he had attempted to resolve it by going a greater distance from home, then the richest and most useful experiences of my own life would have been denied me.

As it was, he not only kept me within the reach and the influence of my native and ancestral ground, he gave me every encouragement, up to and including insistence, to learn everything I could about it. He talked and contrived endlessly to the effect that I should understand the land, not as a commodity, an inert fact to be taken for granted, but as an ultimate value, enduring and alive, useful and beautiful and mysterious and formidable and comforting, beneficent and terribly demanding, worthy of the best of a man's attention and care. With what seems to me to have been, in the face of prevailing fashion and opinion, remarkable insight and foresight, he insisted that I learn to do the hand labor that the land required, knowing—and saying again and again—that the ability to do such work is the source of a confidence and an independence of character that can come no other way, not by money, not by education.

My father was the first, and the most passionate and comprehensive, of my teachers. Too much occupied in town to teach me himself everything he wanted me to know, he saw that I found other teachers. He more or less turned me loose in a landscape populated by teachers: my grandfather and Nick, and many others. He set me free to know a place and a way of life and a kind of people outside the direction, perhaps beyond the scope, and certainly beyond the respect, of the mainstream of the society. Though I am sure he has had to tolerate rather than admire some of the results, it was a great gift.

And so it was by the sanction of my father's sense of things that I made my way between the constricted world of the town and the urban migration and the open world of the fields. And I believe that right at the heart of the better of those worlds, and at the heart of my understanding of it, were the lives of Nick and Aunt Georgie.

Against minds governed by the pragmatism and the egotistical impetus and the secure logic of the drive toward success, a mind such as Aunt Georgie's was a most instructive balance. I suppose that on the evidence that I have given it could be argued that she was ignorant to the point of absurdity and eccentric to the point of craziness. But she was neither absurd nor crazy. She was a woman of formidable dignity and sanity, and her intelligence was *served* by what she knew, or thought she knew, however heterogeneous and unorthodox it may have been. In those days I wanted desperately to share the smug assumptions of my race and class and time that all questions have answers, all problems solutions, all sad stories happy endings. It was good that I should have been tried, that I should have had to contend with Aunt Georgie's unshakable—and accurate—view that life is perilous, surrounded by mystery, acted upon by powerful forces unknown to us. Much as she troubled me and disturbed my sleep, I cannot regret that she told me, bluntly as it needs to be told, that men and events come to strange and painful ends, not foreseen. And whether he exists or not, the hoop snake is only one of a large company of implacable blights that a man might well be prepared to know. And no doubt because of this very darkness of cosmic horror in her mind, everything in the world that she touched became luminous with its own life. She was always *showing* you something: a plant, a bloom, a tomato, an egg, an herb, a sprig of spring greens. Suddenly you saw it as she saw it—vivid, useful, free of all the chances against it, a blessing—and it entered shadowless into your mind. I still keep the deepest sense of delight in the memory of the world's good things held out to me in her black crooked floriferous hands.

And against the anxiety and the greed and the haste and the self-doubt of the white man scrambling for the top, let us place the great serenity and pleasantness of Nick's mind. The supernatural to which Aunt Georgie gave so much of her attention mattered very little to him. For him there was only the Old Marster who required a respectful word or two now and then, but mostly did as He pleased. As for this world, there were two heavy facts that Nick accepted and lived with: life is hard, full of work and pain and weariness, and at the end of it a man has got to go farther than he can imagine from any place he knows. And yet within the confines of those acknowledged facts, he was a man rich in pleasures. They were not large pleasures, they cost little or nothing, often they could not be anticipated, and yet they surrounded him; they were possible at almost any time, or at odd times, or at off times. They were pleasures to which a man had to be acutely and intricately attentive, or he could not have them at all. There were the elemental pleasures of eating and drinking and resting, of being dry while it is raining, of getting dry after getting wet, of getting warm again after getting cold, of cooling off after getting hot. There was pleasure to be taken in good work animals, as long as you remembered the bother and irritation of using the other kind. There was pleasure in the appetites and in the well-being of good animals. There was pleasure in quitting work. There were certain pleasures in the work itself. There was pleasure in hunting and in going to town, and in visiting and in having company. There was pleasure in observing and remembering the behavior of things, and in telling about it. There was pleasure in knowing where a fox lived, and in planning to run it, and in running it. And as I have already made clear, Nick knew how to use his mind for pleasure; he remembered and thought and pondered and imagined. He was a master of what William Carlos Williams called the customs of necessity.

In these times one contemplates it with the same sense of hope with which one contemplates the sunrise or the coming of spring: the image of a man who has labored all his life and will labor to the end, who has no wealth, who owns little, who has no hope of changing, who will never "get somewhere" or "be somebody," and who is yet rich in pleasure, who takes pleasure in the use of his *mind!* Isn't this the very antithesis of the thing that is breaking us in pieces? Isn't there a great rare humane strength in this—this humble possibility that all our effort and aspiration is to deny?

There is, I know, an objection that I will have to face. I can very well imagine being told, there is in my own mind a voice trying to tell me: "You're a fine one to talk! You with your professor's wages, your comfortable house with a furnace and running water and electrical appliances, all the things Nick never had! Who are you to be talking about the pleasures of a poor black man as if they were enviable?"

I have, I think, no way of dealing with this except to leave the question open. I have no way of proving that anything I have said about Nick is true, and I am uncomfortably aware of the dangers and difficulties in a white man's attempt to write so intimately of the life of a black man out of a child's memories a quarter of a century old. I cannot with any assurance claim to know how Nick *was*, but only how he appeared to me, what he meant to me.

About my own present understanding of what I think he meant, I am prepared to be more insistent. This much is clear to me: insofar as I am capable of feeling such pleasures as I believe Nick felt, I am strong; insofar as I am dependent on the pleasures made available by my salary and the things I own, I am weak. I feel much more secure in those pleasures for which I am dependent on the world, as Nick was for most of his, than in those for which I am dependent on the government or on a power company or on the manufacturers of appliances. And I am far from conceding anything to those who assume that the poor or anyone else can be improved by recourse to that carnival of waste and ostentation and greed known as "our high standard of living." As Thoreau so well knew, and so painstakingly tried to show us, what a man most needs is not a knowledge of how to get more, but a knowledge of the most he can do without, and of how to get along without it. The essential cultural discrimination is not between having and not having or haves and have-nots, but between the superfluous and the indispensable. Wisdom, it seems to me, is always poised upon the knowledge of minimums; it might be thought to be the art of minimums. Granting the frailty, and no doubt the impermanence, of modern technology as a human contrivance, the man who can keep a fire in a stove or on a hearth is not only more durable, but wiser, closer to the meaning of fire, than the man who can only work a thermostat.

· *12* ·

If my pattern here has been to depart from my main subject and go back to it, that is because I am attempting to trace, from the influence of two black people I knew as a child, the development of my understanding of the damages of racism, and such an understanding does not grow in a straight or a logical progression from its source. My understanding of the influence of Nick's and Aunt Georgie's minds has been advanced and clarified, as that influence was at first permitted, by the influence of other minds. Also in the last few years my understanding of the general problem of the relations of blacks and whites has been considerably advanced by my own intensified effort to make myself at home in my native place— a task that, past a certain point, is not as easy as might be supposed.

Another difficulty I am aware of is that, by concentrating so exclusively on Nick and Aunt Georgie, I have given the impression that theirs was either the main, or nearly the only, influence which conveyed into my childhood the sense of the countryside and its life—when in fact theirs was only one of many which came to me from blacks *and* whites. That I have thought to ponder at such length over the lives and the influence of two black people is due largely to my growing sense that, in the effort to live meaningfully and decently in America, a white man simply cannot learn all that he needs to know from other American white men. That is because the white man's experience of this continent has so far been incomplete, partly, perhaps mostly, because he has assigned certain critical aspects of the American experience to people he has considered his racial or social inferiors. In my part of America at least racism has made a crucial division between the two races which has produced, as it was bound to do, a crucial difference between them. As the white man has withheld from the black man the positions of responsibility toward the land, and consequently the sense of a legally permanent relationship to it, so he has assigned to him as his proper role the labor, the thousands of menial small acts by which the land is maintained, and by which men develop a closeness to the land and the wisdom of that closeness. For the lack of that closeness and wisdom the white man has suffered and is suffering more than he has admitted, more probably than he knows. It may be the most significant irony in our history that racism, by dividing the two races, has made them not separate but in a fundamental way inseparable, not independent but dependent on each other, incomplete without each other, each needing desperately to understand and make use of the experience of the other. After so much time together we are one body, and the division between us is the disease of one body, not of two. Even the white man and the black man who hate each other are, by that very token, each other's emotional dependents.

A great deal has already been made by various writers of the way white men have attributed to black women the active sexuality that they did not want to see in their own women, because they did not consider sexuality to be ladylike. This is usually discussed with respect to the damage it has done to the pride of the black man and to the relationships of black men and black women. On the other side of the problem, it made the white man by turns either crude or absurdly sentimental in his relationships with the women of his own race, unable to bridge the artificial dichotomy between sex and sentiment in order to know his women as they really are. And it tended to make the white woman of the landed class in the South a functionless ornament, possessing only the powers of prettiness and charm, obsolete by the age of thirty, artificial, pretentious and silly, practicing the manners and the affectations of a world that never did exist and never could have. All that is obvious enough, and so I want only to mention it—adding, however, that the *consequences* of this sexual disorientation go far beyond the considerable unhappiness it has caused to individuals. It has poisoned the very heart of our community. It is as destructive a force as any other that we have let loose.

But there is another effect of racism, in some ways parallel to the one I just mentioned, complexly related to it, and yet different. This one, I think, has not had enough attention paid to it. My own insight into it has its germ in some sentences in an essay by Allen Tate, "The Profession of Letters in the South":

> That *African* chattel slavery was the worst groundwork conceivable for the growth of a great culture of European pattern, is scarcely at this day arguable. Still, as a favorable "culturable situation" it was probably worse than white-chattel, agricultural slavery only in degree. The distance between white master and black slave was unalterably greater than that between white master and white serf after the destruction of feudalism. The peasant *is* the soil. The Negro slave was a barrier between the ruling class and the soil.

I do not share Mr. Tate's assumption that "a great culture of European pattern" was either desirable or possible in America, but I have kept these sentences of his in mind for years and have found them useful. For my own purpose I would like to rephrase the last sentence I quoted as follows: The Negro, both as slave and as servant, has been a barrier between the white people of *all* classes and the soil. And I don't think this was because the Negro was inherently different or alien, as Mr. Tate seems to believe it was, but because of the inferior and menial role which the Negro was assigned.

From the beginning, of course, there have been both white and black laborers; they have often worked side by side; there has often been little economic difference between them. And yet between whites and blacks even as laborers there has been a radical difference both of attitude toward life in the world and of response to the work they had to do. The operative concept in this difference seems to me to have been the white man's idea that certain work was "nigger work."

From the beginning also, as the white man made his drive into the continent, to take it from its wilderness and its original inhabitants and possess it, there were two great necessities: one was to own the land, to establish and maintain a legal claim; the second was the enormous and continuing labor it took to convert such ownership into the profits which would preserve and augment it. In the parts of the country where there was a black labor force these necessities were divided, in theory at least; the white man was to be the owner, the black man was to be the laborer. The black man, even now, rarely crosses into the white man's side of this division. And the white man, though he has unavoidably had to cross over into the black man's side, has never forgotten when he has been there that what he was doing was nigger work. Given the great urgency to own and keep his farm, coupled with the usually wretched economic predicament of the American farmer, it is easy to see why the white owner's interest in the land has usually tended to be abstract, represented in acreages, dollars, measures, numbers. The mind of the white laborer has similarly tended to abstraction; he worked with the idea that his work would lead to ownership, or at least that, as a white man, the nigger work he was doing was unworthy of him; in neither case, because of his sense of racial superiority, did he find it necessary to come to emotional or philosophical terms with the work he was doing. Only the black man, the nigger to whom nigger work was appointed, for whom there was no escape, was able to face it as a present and continuing necessity, and to invent the means of enduring and living with it—and, if I understand the communal and emotional impetus of the work song, of building a culture, not beside or in spite of that necessity, but *upon* it to triumph over it. It seems to me that the black people developed the emotional resilience and equilibrium and the culture necessary to endure and even enjoy hard manual labor wholly aside from the dynamics of ambition. And from this stemmed an ability more complex than that of the white man to know and to bear life. What we should have learned willingly ourselves we *forced* the blacks to learn, and so prevented ourselves from learning it.

There is an enormous difference between working to get some place, for the big payoff that will come later, as the white man does, and working with some serenity and pleasure at the work that is necessary and present, as the black man does, or anyhow as he did. It is the difference between practicality, so-called, and wisdom. Living and responding in terms of present necessities and hardships and pleasures and joys, the blacks have produced an authentic culture in this country, based upon elemental experience; their music has been continuous, responsive to circumstance, and sustaining, from the first work songs and spirituals to the jazz artists in the cities of our own time. Whereas the whites, as a group, have produced here only a pernicious *value system*, based on greed and egotism and the lust for status and comfort, without either an elemental knowledge on the one hand or a decent social vision on the other.

What the whites have produced of cultural value has come into being in the face of either indifference or opposition on the part of most whites; it has been produced by exiles or renegades such as T. S. Eliot and Ezra Pound, or local eccentrics like Henry David Thoreau, Walt Whitman, William Faulkner, and William Carlos Williams.

There are a number of crucial truths, usually ignored, about what we have for so long thought of as nigger work: it is necessary; no society can exist without some form of it; at times it has been done beautifully, as in Japan and in Tuscany, and occasionally even in America; a man who is incapable of it is less than a man, not likely to survive hardships that in the history of the human race are fairly normal; before it encountered the racist mentality the men who did such work and did it well considered themselves dignified by it. The following little poem, coming from a time before our race had decided to use men of other races as gadgets, gives the working man's gleeful sense of his *superiority*:

> When Adam delved and Eve span,
> Who was then the gentleman?

The man who dug and the woman who spun lived at an elemental and independent level; their abilities and their sense of themselves were irreducible; as the author of the poem knew, they could not be brought down by some little political accident, as the gentleman, with his refinements and his inflated self-importance, certainly could.

In relation to the land, then, the role of the white owner has usually been abstract, and the role of the black servant has usually been concrete. Both my grandfather and Nick Watkins worked long hard days all their lives; one could say without fear of injustice to either man that they worked about equally hard. But from that common ground they diverged into radically different attitudes and states of mind. From the first of my grandfather's mature working years to the last, he was never safely beyond the threat of financial ruin. He was always, had *had* to be, deeply concerned with the economic and legal abstractions of landowning, for no matter how well he worked and planned the slant of the market was usually against him. Like many other farmers of his time, he had to contend constantly with a pressure to abuse his land in order to hold on to it. Nick's economic situation, although much lower in fact and in expectancy than my grandfather's, was more stable. In wages I don't believe he ever received more than a dollar a day, but by the usual terms of employment he would also receive meat hogs, feed for his chickens, a house, wood for fuel, the use of a milk cow, and a garden plot. Except that he did not own the land he worked, he practiced a sort of subsistence farming, like his employers living as much as possible off the land. His circumstances did not vary much: from year to year, within the limits of the weather, he received pretty much what he expected. If he was poor, he was not harassed by economic uncertainties or the threat of great economic loss. When my grandfather went to the field his mind was burdened; when Nick went to the field his mind was free. The difference can be illustrated by imagining two figures in a landscape, one of them trying to determine how that landscape can be made to produce the money necessary for the next year's interest, and the other conscious of the whereabouts of the dens of foxes, planning a hunt. And the knowledge I received from those two men is divided in exactly the same way—the two halves, you could say, of a whole relationship to the earth. From my grandfather's struggle to hold on to the land, I got a sense of the continuity of my own people there, their lives invested in the earth, and also the sense of the land as the preserver of such a continuity and of the hope of it; but this had come at the price of a certain estrangement from the very place to which he had joined himself with such passion. From Nick I got a sense of a free intimacy with the place, the possibility of pleasure in *being* there.

It will no doubt seem curious—to some it will no doubt seem outrageous—for me to speak of the black worker as being freer in the landscape than the white owner, and yet I am sure that he very often was. In the landscape, as opposed to the institutions of the white man's society, the black man was simply a man at large with his faculties. Without the economic pressures of ownership, often or even usually doing work which required a minimum of attention, his mind could be free. And it is only in such freedom that the mind becomes intimate with a place, filling itself and delighting in its *details*. In this way the worker and the field he works in become one. It has always been so. Speaking of a company of hired workers, in *Tess of the D'Urbervilles*, Hardy says that "a field woman is a portion of the field; she has somehow lost her own margin . . ." Granting the possibility of subtle differences, the same is true, I think, of a field man.

Early in *The Autobiography of Malcolm X* there occurs this charming passage:

> One thing in particular that I remember made me feel grateful toward my mother was that one day I went and asked her for my own garden, and she did let me have my own little plot. I loved it and took care of it well. I loved especially to grow peas. I was proud when we had them on our table. I would pull out the grass in my garden by hand when the first little blades came up. I would patrol the rows on my hands and knees for any worms and bugs, and I would kill and bury them. And sometimes when I had everything straight and clean for my things to grow, I would lie down on my back between two rows, and I would gaze up into the blue sky at the clouds moving and think all kinds of things.

Malcolm X, it seems to me, was a heroic figure not so much because of what he did, but because of the thorough involvement of a powerful intelligence in all that he did. He had preeminently, as his book shows, the power to assimilate new evidence and new experience, and to change accordingly. He was not, as we were so eager to believe, simply a man of fury; he was a man of *intelligent* fury. He was not simply a creature of his condition or of political struggle, but a man of vision and hope; the pace he kept, I imagine, would itself have soon destroyed a man shallowly motivated. In thinking about the peculiar breadth and depth of Malcolm's intelligence, I keep going back to those few sentences about his garden, not as an explanation but as a clue. Part of the strength of that passage is that it is probably the only really serene and happy moment in the whole book. He doesn't say what were the "all kinds of things" he thought, but it is hard for me to avoid the suspicion that the experience—lying there as low as he could get, against the earth, his mind free—filled him with a rich sense of the possibilities of life in this world that never left him, and that served him as a measure of the destructiveness and sterility of racism. The passage throws the resonance of myth over the book: it is the myth of Antaeus, the giant of Libya, the son of Earth, who could not be conquered so long as he touched the ground.

· *13* ·

For a long time after I was grown the question of racism remained passive in me. I subscribed to the principles of political equality and civil rights. I had not knowingly mistreated or insulted any black person because he was black. I hoped, in a general way, that the "race situation" would be solved in a manner that would be acceptable and beneficial to the Negroes. On the other hand, I was not really dealing with the question. I think I lacked any clarifying or critical sense of my own involvement in the problems and the costs of racism.

For several years I lived in what seems to me now to have been a very *general* way. My major aim was to keep writing, and I had done so by taking advantage of random opportunities, traveling here and there, living a year or two in one place and a year or two in another. And then in the spring of 1964 I turned back on the direction I had been going. I returned to Kentucky, and within a year bought and moved onto a little farm in my native part of the state.

That return made me finally an exile from the ornamental Europeanism that still passes for culture with most Americans. What I had done caused my mind to be thrown back forcibly upon its sources: my home countryside, my own people and history. And for the first time I felt my nakedness. I realized that the culture I needed was not to be found by visiting museums and libraries and auditoriums. It occurred to me that there was another measure for my life than the amount or even the quality of the writing I did; a man, I thought, must be judged by how willingly and meaningfully he can be present where he is, by how fully he can make himself at home in his part of the world. I began to want desperately to learn to belong to my place. The test, it seemed to me, would be how content I could become to remain in it, how independent I could be, there, of other places.

Conceptually, the question of nativeness and of the sense of belonging to a place is arbitrary, as birth is arbitrary. It is also subjective. This is what chauvinism ignores; one's place cannot be proven to be the best in the world. Given the fact of birth in a place, belonging there is a matter of ecological adjustment *after* the fact. Living in a place from birth, one becomes a part of its life. I wanted to live in my native place for the same reason that the bloodroot of our woods is to be found in our woods and not on prairies. It is not defensible, only demonstrable.

I have said enough earlier, perhaps, to suggest the web of memory and association that provided the particular terms of my allegiance to my native place. But having returned to that place and resumed its life, I began to feel at the same time a deep estrangement from it. Going day after day about the work of my little farm, I began to have a sense of the thousands of acts, properly honored and understood generation after generation, that are necessary to surround a man with a culture sufficient to his life in a given place. In such a culture a man's every act would be as ritualistic, as rich in association, as aware of being a repetition of previous acts, as the agriculture of peasantries and Indian tribes.

I became thoughtful of all the work that had been done there on my home ground either by despised men or by men who secretly despised themselves for doing the work of despised men—so many of the necessary acts of my history, neither valued nor understood, wasted in the process of wasting the earth. And I thought back to the time before the brief violent spasm of my people's history there, to the thousands of years when the Shawnees and their forebears lived in the country in its maidenhood, familiar with it as they were with their own bodies, as much at home in it as the plants and animals, wedded to it by an exquisite awareness of its life. They were native as no one has been since. And I began to understand how the racism of my people has been a barrier not just between us and our land but between us and our exemplary predecessors.

———

It is not out of the abstract ministrations of priests and teachers from outside the immediate life of a place that the ceremonies of atonement with the creation arise, but out of the thousand small acts, repeated year after year and generation after generation, by which men relate to their soil. Going out to plant and to cultivate and to harvest again and again, as one's father went out and his father before him, the sense of familiarity finally crests in ritual—exactly as work rhythms build into work *songs*—which tends not only to protect the individual's sense of himself in relation to the place, but to protect the place as well.

Our politics and science have never mastered the fact that people need more than to understand their obligation to one another and to the earth; they need also the *feeling* of such obligation, and the feeling can come only within the patterns of familiarity. A nation of urban nomads, such as we have become, may simply be unable to be enough disturbed by its destruction of the ecological health of the land, because the people's dependence on the land, though it has been *expounded* to them over and over again in general terms, is not immediate to their feelings. I believe that it is psychologically necessary that people develop, in addition to the forms by which to enact the duties prescribed by their relationships to each other and to the earth, the forms by which to enact their *consciousness* of these relationships. It seems to me that among a genuinely native and settled people the practical forms of daily and seasonal tasks would culminate finally in the forms of religion, and that the concourses between the lowliest and the most exalted forms would be familiar and open and direct. In such a situation a person would not consider himself to be involved in a series of abstract relationships, as one of a number, but a conscious responsible participant in the life both of the land he lived from and of the universe, dependent upon the greater life but also its protector. From what I have read I gather that the American Indian did not conceive of himself as a mechanically producing and consuming agent of a political compact, but as the spiritual heir of the life of the creation. He was the agent and legator of this life, but also a part of it, and his religion was the enactment of his unity with it. The superb grace of his realization of this oneness is given in John Collier's description of one of the sacred dances of the Pueblos:

> The occasion as a whole was a summoning by the tribe of many spirits of the wild, elements or cosmic kin known from ages gone by; and a summoning from within the breast of capacities and loves which had formed the ancient life and must sustain its present and future. As the hours moved on, a displacement of human and mystical factors seemed to take place. The rejoicing was not only a human rejoicing; and that marvelous ever-renewed, ever-increasing, ever-changing leap and rush of song was not only human song. A threshold had been

shifted, forces of the wild and of the universe had heard the call and
had taken the proffered dominion. That is what the tribe believed;
that is how it seemed . . .

Like other parts of the country, Kentucky is full of places, once
settled and farmed at a great expenditure of time and labor, that are
now abandoned; after only a few generations a whole human era
has come to an end there. I know of many such places myself—hilly
land, for the most part, with narrow creek bottoms. The families
came there, cleared the woods off the land, built houses and barns
and miles of stone fence, dug wells, and then in only a few decades
gave it all up; they had worn the land out.

It would be a great mistake to assume that this happened because
those were marginal places to begin with, and that it was thus inevitable that human life could not maintain itself in them for long.
They were, many of them, rich enough in the beginning. The people
could not remain in those places because their relation to them was
mechanical and economic rather than cultural. They lacked the
cultural means which might have provided the knowledge either of
the importance of preserving the land or of the right ways to preserve it.

It was not necessary that these lands should have been destroyed.
It is certain that our destructiveness will not stop with their destruction. We have given ourselves no good reason not to see in these desolate places the future of the whole country.

· *14* ·

It seems to me that racism could not possibly have made merely a mechanical division between the two races; at least in America it did not. It involves an emotional dynamics that has disordered the heart both of the society as a whole and of every person in the society. It has made divisions not only between white people and black people, but between black men and black women, white men and white women; it has come between white people and their work, and between white people and their land. It has fragmented both our society and our minds.

Now we are surrounded by signs that this fragmentation has reached some sort of limit. The convention or the inertia or whatever it is that has held the pieces together for so long is beginning to give way. The agony of racism, not only that of the blacks, but our own which we have taken such care to hide, is becoming too clear to be ignored or denied.

My feeling is that in the people of each race there is a longing, either conscious or unconscious, to be accepted and liked by people of the other race; there is the intuition that such a liking of people for each other would tear away the centuries of hypocrisy and lies, and enfranchise our best hopes. But we have a lot standing in our way. At a time when the stupidity and destructiveness of racism is more apparent than ever, people seem to be more racially conscious than ever. The blacks know harsher truths about the whites than the whites have ever admitted to themselves—and the whites know it. No matter how friendly a given white may *seem*, the black man, of course, fears that he is being stereotyped and misjudged. Whites fear what they feel, secretly or otherwise, to be the righteousness of the anger of the blacks; as the oppressors they feel, secretly or otherwise, morally inferior to those they have oppressed. In their struggle to advance themselves, the blacks fear to be disarmed by the proffered friendliness of whites. It is even possible for whites to hesitate to offer friendliness to blacks for fear that they will seem to condescend or patronize. And in many places the two races are now divided more than ever, and are less known to each other. Where they have withdrawn into the ghettos of white and black they know each other only as abstractions; they are more divided than they were at the time of slavery. This does not merely intensify the crisis; it may well be that this *is* the crisis.

The crucial difference, I think, between our society and others that have been divided, by class if not by race, is that in our self-protective silence up to now about the whole problem, we have not developed the language by which to recognize the extent or the implications of the division, and we have not developed either the language or the necessary social forms by which to recognize across the division our common interest and our common humanity. For this reason I have been thinking back to passages in books I have read that deal with the meeting and mutual recognition of social opposites.

The most ancient example of such a meeting that I have thought of, and the most ceremonious, the one most intricately prepared for in its culture, is in the *Odyssey*, when Odysseus is entertained by the swineherd Eumaios. Odysseus has just set foot on Ithaka, his home island, for the first time in twenty years. Disguised as a stranger and not recognized by Eumaios, Odysseus is welcomed by the swineherd as a guest. He is given food and drink and a place to sleep at Eumaios' hearth. Odysseus is a king, the lord of the island, and Eumaios is a lowly peasant charged with looking after the pigs, and yet Homer seems to give to their meeting a supreme importance. Eumaios is the first man Odysseus meets when he lands on the island, and he accompanies him to the end, until the life of the island is made orderly again, through all the concentric circles of its moral structure, from the sea coast to the returned king's marriage bed. There are other ways by which Homer indicates the importance of Eumaios (he seems *personally* to have liked him better than any other character except Odysseus); for instance he calls him "the noble swineherd" and "the glorious swineherd." These epithets, the general tone of respect for Eumaios, the importance of his role, all seem to me to imply a certain equality between the servant and the hero, if not of person then of function; it is as if Homer is saying that the health of the kingdom depends fully as much on the faithfulness of its servants as it does on the faithfulness of its king. Indeed, the two figures represent not only the opposite ends of the social scale, but two opposite, and mutually sustaining, kinds of faithfulness: Odysseus' is the faithfulness which ventures and returns; Eumaios' that which remains and preserves. As the faithful servant Eumaios represents and speaks for the homeland; he is in charge of the ceremonies of hospitality and welcome. Odysseus' dependence, the idea that the king is incomplete in himself, is symbolized in that he first returns to his kingdom as the guest of his servant. If Odysseus may be said to represent the questing spirit, then Eumaios represents the order without which questing would be too

costly or impossible; he is generous and ceremonious, as opposed
to the suitors "who have no regard for anyone in their minds."

There is another, more subtle and ironic suggestion in Homer's
representation of the king and the swineherd as equals. The poet, I
think, is using this meeting to make clear that it is not as a king that
Odysseus survives his ordeal, and returns to reorder his kingdom,
but as a man reduced to the narrowest definition of manhood. As
the two men talk by the fire they are, in material terms, literally
equals, for Odysseus at that point has lost everything. If he is a better man than Eumaios, more deserving to be a king, it is not because
of his hereditary right, but because he has survived more and by that
survival is proven wiser; he is a greater master of the customs of necessity; he has been capable of kingly behavior within the minimum
estate of manhood.

This passage is not, of course, relevant to our dilemma in the
sense that it provides any idea or pattern for social change. Homer
was apparently satisfied with the class structure of Ithaka, and he
makes it clear that Eumaios was good insofar as he was a good *servant*. But it does testify in no uncertain terms that a divided society
is made up of fragments, incomplete in themselves, and it provides
us an example of a social form by which people who represent opposite social halves may recognize and honor each other as human
beings.

The nearest we have come in our literature to such a meeting is in
the relationship of Jim and Huck Finn on their voyage down the
Mississippi. This relationship changes, clarifying itself finally in
terms of the deepest humanity, in the course of a terrible struggle in
Huck's mind between his conscience, which tells him that Jim is
property and therefore should be returned to slavery, and his feelings which tell him that Jim is both a man and a beloved friend.

The crisis begins when Huck, automatically treating Jim as a nigger, plays him a cruel joke. And with all the dignity of outraged justice Jim rebukes him: "Dat truck dah is *trash*; en trash is what people is dat puts dirt on de head er dey frens en makes 'em ashamed." And Huck, feeling for the first time the *claims* of Jim's humanity, is humbled, and as he usually does he makes an honest response:

> It was fifteen minutes before I could work myself up to go and humble myself to a nigger; but I done it, and I warn't ever sorry for it afterwards, neither. I didn't do him no more mean tricks, and I wouldn't have done that one if I'd a knowed it would make him feel that way.

Later, prodded by his "conscience," Huck starts out to betray Jim, and then at the last moment falters, thinking of their friendship, and backs out.

The crisis is not completely resolved until much later, and then it is resolved in the most final of terms. In another seizure of guilt at helping "a nigger to get his freedom," Huck writes a note to Jim's owner, Miss Watson, telling her where Jim can be found. And then again he thinks of his and Jim's friendship and of their history together. And he looks back at the note:

> It was a close place. I took it up, and held it in my hand. I was a-trembling, because I'd got to decide, forever, betwixt two things, and I knowed it. I studied a minute, sort of holding my breath, and then says to myself:
> "All right, then, I'll *go* to hell"—and tore it up.

Given the vividness of hell to the mind of such a boy as Huck, the scene has a cosmic scale and finality. Huck not only makes an unequivocal allegiance to Jim as a man, but he commits himself to that allegiance to the limits of his imagination; he ratifies his sense of Jim's humanity by the greatest imaginable self-sacrifice. It is a profoundly wakeful and anguished moment in the history of the American conscience.

But its limitations must also be recognized. Whereas the *Odyssey* represents the maturity of the moral consciousness of a whole people, *Huckleberry Finn* shows only its *beginnings* in the mind of a child. And with a self-protective dexterity that would not have surprised Mark Twain in the least, the adult racist mentality of America has dealt with the threat of that beginning by decreeing that *Huckleberry Finn* is not a book for the chastening of adults, which to a large extent it certainly is, but a book for the entertainment of children.

I know of two other scenes in which representatives of the two halves of a sharply divided society meet. Both of them are from Tolstoy. It seems important to me that the participants in these meetings are adults.

In *Anna Karenina*, Konstantin Levin, an aristocratic landowner much like Tolstoy, decides to go out into the fields to mow with the peasants. He tells his brother, who replies:

> "But what will you do about eating with them? To send you a bottle of Château Lafite and roast turkey out there would be a little awkward."

But in spite of his embarrassment at abandoning his conventional role, Levin spends a long day mowing with a scythe at the side of an old peasant who becomes his mentor. As the day goes on, Levin gradually understands and masters the work; he gets the *feel* of it. And from the understanding of the work itself, he comes to understand the kind of mind produced by such work. The mind of the old peasant, far from being that of a benighted drudge (cf. Edwin Markham's "The Man with the Hoe"), is a mind intensely alive, humorous, attentive to the life going on around him. From the old peasant's mind Levin gets a sense of the intricacy and beauty of the life of the meadow that could not possibly have come to him in his role of landlord:

> The longer Levin mowed, the oftener he felt the moments of uncon-sciousness in which it seemed that the scythe was mowing by itself, a body full of life and consciousness of its own, and as though by magic, without thinking of it, the work turned out regular and precise by it-self. These were the most blissful moments.
>
> It was hard work only when he had to break off the motion, which had become unconscious, and think; when he had to mow around a mound or a tuft of sorrel. The old man did this easily. When a mound came, he changed his action, and at one time with the heel, at another with the tip of his scythe, he clipped the mound around both sides with short strokes. And while he did this he kept looking about and watching what came into his view: at one moment he picked a wild berry and ate it or offered it to Levin, then he flung away a twig with the blade of the scythe, then he looked at a quail's nest, from which the bird flew just under the scythe, or caught a snake that crossed his path and, lifting it on the scythe as though on a fork, showed it to Levin and threw it away.

In Levin's day at work with the peasants there is no condescen-sion; he is not slumming. He undertakes the work because he is at-tracted to it, and in the doing of it his mind breaks out of the class boundaries and arrives at a vital sense of the life of a man unlike himself. He becomes an initiate of the other life. At dinnertime all this is acknowledged by the old peasant, who invites Levin to eat with him:

> "Come, master, taste my grub," said he, kneeling down before the cup.
>
> The food was so good that Levin gave up the idea of going home. He dined with the old man, and talked to him about his family affairs, taking the keenest interest in them, and told him about his own affairs

and all the circumstances that could be of interest to the old man. He felt much closer to him than to his brother, and could not help smiling at the affection he felt for this man.

But by far the most complex and articulate and conscious of these encounters occurs in *War and Peace*. Pierre Bezúkhov, the intellectual and aristocrat, Russian by birth but European in culture and education, is taken prisoner by the French after their invasion of Moscow. The episode that follows develops as a ritual of spiritual death and rebirth.

Certain that he has been sentenced to death, Pierre is led with other prisoners to a place called Virgin's Field. There the prisoners are placed in order, according to a list, and the first five are shot. Pierre, who is sixth in line, is spared. But he is nevertheless badly damaged in spirit:

> From the moment Pierre had witnessed those terrible murders committed by men who did not wish to commit them, it was as if the mainspring of his life, on which everything depended and which made everything appear alive, had suddenly been wrenched out and everything had collapsed into a heap of meaningless rubbish. Though he did not acknowledge it to himself, his faith in the right ordering of the universe, in humanity, in his own soul, and in God, had been destroyed.

That night he is taken to a prison barracks where, as he sits in despondency, he becomes aware of a man sitting beside him who smells strongly of sweat. The stranger is taking off his leg bands and in other ways making himself comfortable for the night, and there comes to Pierre an awareness of "something pleasant, comforting, and well rounded in these deft movements, in the man's well-ordered arrangements . . ."

This man is Platón Karatáev, a peasant who has been serving as a soldier. He speaks kindly to Pierre, gives him a potato to eat, calls him "dear lad." His speech is full of old sayings, the wisdom of the peasant culture. "I say things happen not as we plan but as God judges," he says. And: "The great thing is to live in harmony . . ." Of the burning of Moscow he says: "the maggot gnaws the cabbage, yet dies first." In the most depressing circumstances he is buoyant and generous; there is an immutable serenity in him that accepts facts as facts. He lies down and prays, "Lay me down like a stone, O God, and raise me up like a loaf," and falls asleep:

> Sounds of crying and screaming came from somewhere in the distance outside, and flames were visible through the cracks of the shed, but inside it was quiet and dark. For a long time Pierre did not sleep, but lay with eyes open in the darkness, listening to the regular snoring of Platón who lay beside him, and he felt that the world that had been shattered was once more stirring in his soul with a new beauty and on new and unshakable foundations.

Platón Karatáev is simple and saintly, wise not in his own intelligence but in the intelligence of the peasant culture that he inherits. He is enduring, adequate to the demands of the worst that can happen to him. He is yet another master of the customs of necessity, the minute strategies of endurance and of joy:

> He could do everything, not very well, but not badly. He baked, cooked, sewed, planed, and mended boots. He was always busy, and only at night allowed himself conversation—of which he was fond—and songs. He did not sing like a trained singer who knows he is listened to, but like the birds, evidently giving vent to the sounds in the same way that one stretches oneself or walks about to get rid of stiffness . . .

He is spiritually free:

> Karatáev had no attachments, friendships, or loves, as Pierre understood them, but loved and lived affectionately with everything life

brought him in contact with, particularly with man—not any particular man, but those with whom he happened to be. He loved his dog, his comrades, the French, and Pierre who was his neighbor, but Pierre felt that in spite of Karatáev's affectionate tenderness for him (by which he unconsciously gave Pierre's spiritual life its due) he would not have grieved for a moment at parting from him. And Pierre began to feel in the same way toward Karatáev.

Karatáev is at one both with his own life and with that of the world. In his simple-hearted comprehension of complex truths, he is a spokesman not for himself but for the Russian peasantry and the peasantry's long and intricate experience of the land of Russia. Karatáev's is the voice of the land of Russia:

> Sometimes Pierre, struck by the meaning of his words, would ask him to repeat them, but Platón could never recall what he had said a moment before, just as he never could repeat to Pierre the words of his favorite song: *native* and *birch tree* and *my heart is sick* occurred in it, but when spoken and not sung, no meaning could be got out of it. He did not, and could not, understand the meaning of words apart from their context. Every word and action of his was the manifestation of an activity unknown to him, which was his life. But his life, as he regarded it, had no meaning as a separate thing. It had meaning only as part of a whole of which he was always conscious. His words and actions flowed from him as evenly, inevitably, and spontaneously as fragrance exhales from a flower. He could not understand the value or significance of any word or deed taken separately.

Until he has made spiritual contact with the wisdom of his homeland and its indigenous people, the peasants, all of Pierre's European learning is for nothing, a wandering in the wilderness. Until he stands in his own eyes not as a count but as a man, possessed only of what he has in common with all men, he can know neither peace nor joy.

Tolstoy indicates the great change in Pierre's spirit by describing the change in his appearance:

Pierre's attire now consisted of a dirty torn shirt . . . a pair of soldier's trousers which by Karatáev's advice he tied with string round the ankles for warmth, and a peasant coat and cap . . . The former slackness which had shown itself even in his eyes was now replaced by an energetic readiness for action and resistance. His feet were bare.

It is not as an aristocrat, then, that Pierre survives his ordeal, but as a peasant. As such, he can endure his trial "not only lightly but joyfully," for his condition has forced him to fall back, peasantlike, upon the elemental pleasures:

Here and now for the first time he fully appreciated the enjoyment of eating when he wanted to eat, drinking when he wanted to drink, sleeping when he wanted to sleep, of warmth when he was cold, of talking to a fellow man when he wished to talk and to hear a human voice.

And he feels a new sense of communion with the natural life of the world of which he is a part:

When on the first day he got up early, went out of the shed at dawn, and saw the cupolas and crosses of the New Convent of the Virgin still dark at first, the hoarfrost on the dusty grass, the Sparrow Hills, and the wooded banks above the winding river vanishing in the purple distance, when he felt the contact of the fresh air and heard the noise of the crows flying from Moscow across the field, and when afterwards light gleamed from the east and the sun's rim appeared solemnly from behind a cloud, and the cupolas and crosses, the hoarfrost, the distance and the river, all began to sparkle in the glad light—Pierre felt a new joy and strength in life such as he had never before known. And this not only stayed with him during the whole of his imprisonment, but even grew in strength as the hardships of his position increased.

All this leads to the religious affirmation which comes to him in a dream on the retreat. It is an affirmation which conforms exactly to the faith of Karatáev, as symbolized in the peasant's inability to understand things separately:

> "Life is everything. Life is God. Everything changes and moves and that movement is God. And while there is life there is joy in consciousness of the divine. To love life is to love God. Harder and more blessed than all else is to love this life in one's sufferings, in innocent suffering."

· *15* ·

Those four scenes, placed in the context of the contemporary racial crisis in America, seem to me richly suggestive. They supply, out of history and out of other cultures, a sense of human contact and allegiance that balances and amplifies my own memories of my friendship with Nick and Aunt Georgie.

All of these scenes are written out of the awareness that divisions of class or race within a society are not superficial, but have the most profound spiritual effect both on the society and on the individuals in it. The writers say or imply that men on *both* sides of these divisions suffer because of them, and that only in the healing of the divisions are they made whole.

They testify in one way or another to the value of what might be called the underview, the ground-level perspective of those at the bottom of the social structure. Those who are higher up are not only dependent on those below them but, cut off from them by social convention, are denied the elemental experience and the elemental wisdom available only to those in immediate free contact with the earth.

The passages from Homer and Tolstoy affirm that one man alone does not have strength or dignity or joy, but that these and all else that is worthy come to him by the grace of the bonds that he has made with his fellows, and out of his sense of belonging to his land. They tell us, as biologists in our own time are again telling us, that no man is alone, because *he cannot be*; he cannot arrange it so that either the good or the bad effects of his life will apply only to himself; he can only live in the creation, among the creatures, his life either adding to the commonwealth or subtracting from it. Men are whole not only insofar as they make common cause with each other, but also insofar as they make common cause with their native earth, which is to say with the creation as a whole, which is to say with the creator.

And perhaps most important of all, these four encounters testify that the real healings and renewals in human life occur in individual *lives*, not in the process of adjusting or changing their abstractions or their institutions. Such meetings as that of Huck and Jim or that of Pierre and Platón Karatáev have a tremendous power to change men's lives and, as a consequence, their relations with other men. Without such change as this, institutional changes become merely the occasions of hypocrisy. These are in the best sense *instructive* texts, and their aim is revolution of a sort. But they are not political texts. They are not interested in the superficial revolutions by which men change their politics; they are interested in the profound metamorphoses that occur when men "rectify their hearts." No matter what laws or governments say, men can only know and come to care for one another by meeting face to face, arduously, and by the willing loss of comfort.

I believe that the experience of all honest men stands, like these books, against the political fantasy that deep human problems can be satisfactorily solved by legislation. On the contrary, it is likely that the best and least oppressive laws come as the result or the reflection of honest solutions that men have already made in their own lives. The widespread assumption that men can be set free or dignified or improved by monkeying with some mere aspect or manifestation of their lives—politics or economics or technology—promises no solution, but only an unlimited growth of the public apparatus. The American people may solve their problems themselves, and so save the world a catastrophe, but not by insisting that the government do their work for them. No man will ever be whole and dignified and free except in the knowledge that the men around him are whole and dignified and free, and that the world itself is free of contempt and misuse.

For want of the sense of such freedom, even as an ideal, the white race in America has marketed and destroyed more of the fertility of the earth in less time than any other race that ever lived. In my part of the country, at least, this is largely to be accounted for by the racial division of the *experience* of the landscape. The white man, preoccupied with the abstractions of the economic exploitation and ownership of the land, necessarily has lived on the country as a destructive force, an ecological catastrophe, because he assigned the hand labor, and in that the possibility of intimate knowledge of the land, to a people he considered racially inferior; in thus debasing labor, he destroyed the possibility of a meaningful contact with the earth. He was literally blinded by his presuppositions and prejudices. Because he did not know the land, it was inevitable that he would squander its natural bounty, deplete its richness, corrupt and pollute it, or destroy it altogether. The history of the white man's use of the earth in America is a scandal. The history of his effort to build here what Allen Tate calls "a great culture of European pattern" is a farce. To farm here, as we have done for centuries, as if the land and the climate were European, has been ruinous, ecologically and agriculturally, and no doubt culturally as well.

(To the credit of the white man's ideal of ownership, it must be said that it did for a time foster in this country a population of independent small farmers which, in spite of the crudity and wastefulness of some of its methods, was one of the hopeful accomplishments of our system. Jefferson recognized the value of these people, and spoke for them. Today, because of the machines and the corporations and the middlemen and predatory markets and public contempt for their role, they are nearly extinct.)

The notion that one is too good to do what it is necessary for *somebody* to do is always weakening. The unwillingness, or the inability, to dirty one's hands in one's own service is a serious flaw of character. But in a society that sense of superiority can cut off a whole class or a whole race from its most necessary experience. For one thing, it can curtail or distort a society's sense of the means, and of the importance of the means, of getting work done; it prolongs and ramifies the life and effect of pernicious abstractions. In America, for instance, one of the most depraved and destructive habits has always been an obsession with results. Getting the job done is good. Pondering as to how the job should be done, or whether or not it should be done, is apt to be regarded as a waste of time. If we want coal, it seems to us perfectly feasible to destroy a mountain or a valley in order to get it. If we want to "contain Communism," we do not hesitate to do so by destroying the "threatened" country. Today we send a bulldozer or a bomber to do our dirty work as casually, and by the same short-order morality, as once (in the South) we would "send a nigger," or (in the North) an Irishman, or (in the West now) a Mexican.

The abstractness of the white man's relation to the land has forced the black man to develop resources of character and religion and art that have some resemblance to the peasant cultures of the old world—Nick Watkins, it seems to me, had a good deal in common with Platón Karatáev—but at the same time it has denied him the peasant's sense of a permanent relation to the earth. He has wandered off the land into the cities in the hope of being better treated, only to be scorned as before. And on the land his place has been taken by machines—and we are more estranged from our land now than we ever were.

For examples of a whole and indigenous American society, functioning in full meaning and good health within the ecology of this continent, we will have to look back to the cultures of the Indians. That we failed to learn from them how to live in this land is a stupidity—a *racial* stupidity—that will corrode the heart of our society until the day comes, if it ever does, when we do turn back to learn from them. Inheriting the cultural growth of thousands of years, they had a responsible sense of living within the creation—which is to say that they had, among much else, an ecological morality—and a complex awareness of the life of their land which we have hardly begun to have. They had a cultural and spiritual wholeness of which the white and black races have so far had only the divided halves.

Empowered by technology, the abstractions of the white man's domination of the continent threaten now to annihilate the specific characteristics of all races, virtues and vices alike, absorbing them as neutral components into a machine society. It is, then, not simply a question of black power or white power, but of how meaningfully to reenfranchise *human* power. This, as I think Martin Luther King understood, is the real point, the real gift to America, of the struggle of the black people. In accepting the humanity of the black race, the white race will not be giving accommodation to an alien people; it will be receiving into itself half of its own experience, vital and indispensable to it, which it has so far denied at great cost.

As soon as we have fulfilled the hollow in our culture, the silence in our speech, with the fully realized humanity of the black man—and it follows, of the American Indian—then there will appear over the horizon of our consciousness another figure as well: that of the American white man, our *own* humanity, lost to us these three and a half centuries, the time of all our life on this continent.

It is not, I think, a question of when and how the white people will "free" the black and the red people. It is a condescension to believe that we have the power to do that. Until we have recognized in them the full strength and grace of their distinctive humanity we will be able to set no one free, for we will not be free ourselves. When we realize that they possess a knowledge for the lack of which we are incomplete and in pain, then the wound in our history will be healed. Then they will simply *be* free, among us—and so will we, among ourselves for the first time, and among them.

Afterword

I wrote *The Hidden Wound* in the Bender Room of the Stanford University library during the Christmas holiday of 1968–1969. It was a pleasant time of work. The students were gone; the campus was quiet; as I wrote, woodpeckers flew busily past the windows, storing acorns under the roof tiles.

The book was conceived and written under the influence of the civil rights agitation of the time as I was experiencing it around me at Stanford. The immediate issue on the campus was the establishment of a black studies program, but the issues talked about were mainly national and abstract. I attended a number of outdoor meetings called by campus blacks at, I believe, the noon hour. The blacks, mostly young, sat or stood along a low stone wall, confronting an audience of whites, faculty and students, who sat on the grass. The blacks, one by one, accused and berated the whites, sometimes addressing them by obscene epithets, and the whites cheered and applauded. Speakers and hearers seemed to be in perfect agreement that the whites were absolutely guilty of racism, and that the blacks were absolutely innocent of it. They were thus absolutely divided by their agreement.

Another incident from that time has stayed in my mind. A friend and I were walking through the cloister of the Quadrangle when we were suddenly met and forced out of the way by what turned out to be a civil rights protest. I said to my friend, "What's going on?" Whereupon one of the marchers, a young white man, turned and said to me in utter fury: "You damned well better find out!" I suppose that my southern (i.e., north central Kentucky) speech had identified me to him as a racist.

Though I was not a racist, I was fully aware that I belonged to the history of racism and had the influence of it in me. I felt that I had a stake in the outcome. And so I observed these encounters with interest—indeed, with fascination. It was obvious that the presence of such feelings in the nation could not be without political results, and that the results might be to some extent good. But the implicit agreement on the historical scheme of white guilt and black innocence, white victory and black defeat, seemed hopeless to me. In this public life of the issues of racism and civil rights, one felt the possibility of an agreement of sorts, but nowhere the possibility of the mutual recognition of a common humanity, or the possibility of forgiveness and reconciliation, or the possibility of love. If love was present at those public meetings, it was the self-love of self-righteous anger and the self-love of self-righteous guilt.

I did not speak at any of those meetings, and I cannot imagine how I might have done so. They did, however, cause me to want to say something too complicated and laborious to say at a public meeting then, or perhaps now. I wanted to say that, though I knew that American racism had put whites and blacks into the roles of oppressors and oppressed, I had not experienced it as a victory for the oppressor. I knew well that racism had caused pain to black people, but I knew too that it had been a cause of pain to white people—it had been a cause of pain to me—and not just because of guilt. I knew that for white people it had involved loss and spiritual disfigurement. And I knew, from my own experience, that it had involved love.

And so, when my teaching duties were over at the end of the fall quarter, I sat down at a long table between two bookcases in the Bender Room to try to say my own piece.

————

An essay about a social problem does not allow the writer's satisfaction as an expectable result, and *The Hidden Wound* is in some ways the least satisfying essay that I have written. Such an essay, to begin with, can hope to be only a tiny part of a conversation; this particular conversation was old when I entered it, and will be much older before it is concluded. The passages in which I attempted to think about the problem of racism are, therefore, necessarily inconclusive. The passages of remembrance and tribute seem to me by far the most satisfactory. Also the problem seemed to me more difficult when I reached the end of the book than when I began, and I am sorry that it is not more clearly informed by my growing awareness of the difficulty.

In the nearly twenty years since the book was written, my sense of the difficulty has increased still more, partly because I think the difficulty itself has increased. Between the death of Martin Luther King and now, much has happened in the story of the American races, and some improvement has been made. In 1988 a black man has been a strong contender for the Democratic party's presidential nomination—something that would have been unthinkable in 1968.

And yet such improvement has occurred in a country that, by other measures, has been in serious and worsening disarray. The presidential race in which Jesse Jackson has figured so prominently has been perceived by most of the electorate, and rightly so, as a bore. It is a bore, necessarily, because the candidates are not discussing the causes of our malaise: the widening rift between rich and poor, the decline in the ownership of useful property, the cost and influence of public and private debt, the rising costs to individuals and to our society and country of the present versions of scientific and economic "progress," the implications of nuclear power for war or peace, the decline of public education into baby sitting, job training, or incarceration. Of all the candidates, Jesse Jackson alone has spoken for the poor and the dispossessed, and no one has spoken for the country itself against our national habits of land-rape and pollution.

———

When I wrote *The Hidden Wound* in 1968, I did not see how the freedom and prosperity of the people could be separated as issues from the issue of the health of the land, and I still do not. I wrote the book because it seemed to me that the psychic wound of racism had resulted inevitably in wounds in the land, the country itself. I believed then, and I believe more strongly now, that the root of our racial problem in America is not racism. The root is in our inordinate desire to be superior—not to some inferior or subject people, though this desire leads to the subjection of people—but to our condition. We wish to rise above the sweat and bother of taking care of anything—of ourselves, of each other, or of our country. We did not enslave African blacks because they were black, but because their labor promised to free us of the obligations of stewardship, and because they were unable to prevent us from enslaving them. They were economically valuable and militarily weak.

It seems likely, then, that what we now call racism came about as a justification of slavery after the fact, not as its cause. We decided that blacks were inferior in order to persuade ourselves that it was all right to enslave them. That this is true is suggested by our present treatment of other social groups to whom we assign the laborious jobs of caretaking. For it is not only the racial minorities who receive our indifference or contempt, but economic or geographic minorities as well. Anyone who has been called "redneck" or "hillbilly" or "hick" or sometimes even "country person" or "farmer" shares with racial minorities the experience of a stigmatizing social prejudice. And such terms as "redneck" and "hillbilly" and "hick" have remained acceptable in public use long after the repudiation of such racial epithets as "nigger" and "greaser." "Rednecks" and "hillbillies" and "hicks" are scorned because they do what used to be known as "nigger work"—work that is fundamental and inescapable. And it should not be necessary to point out the connection between the oppression of women and the general contempt for household work. It is well established among us that you may hold up your head in polite society with a public lie in your mouth or other people's money in your pocket or innocent blood on your hands, but not with dishwater on your hands or mud on your shoes.

What we did not understand at the time of slavery, and understand poorly still, is that this presumption of the inferiority of economic groups is a contagion that we cannot control, for the presumed inferiority of workers inevitably infects the quality of their work, which inevitably infects the quality of the work place, which is to say the quality of the country itself. When a nation determines that the work of providing and caretaking is "nigger work" or work for "hillbillies" or "rednecks"—that is, fundamental, necessary, inescapable, *and inferior*—then it has implanted in its own soul the infection of its ruin.

The opprobrium implied in the term "nigger work" was, of course, not a problem confined below the Ohio River. The overriding aim of Yankee ingenuity, to this day, has been "freedom from drudgery." The great motive and the great "selling point" of industrialism has been "less work." Our national goal, indeed, has been less work, and we have succeeded. Most people who work are now working less or with less effort (and skill) than they once did, and increasing numbers are not working at all.

That this "less work" has inescapably implied poorer work, poorer products, and unhealthy side-effects is a fact not yet on the agenda of presidential debate. The great persons of politics are no better equipped than the average citizen to compute the costs of "less work," though they, like the average citizen, must spend their leisure time in breathing poisonous air.

The problem of race, nevertheless, is generally treated as if it could be solved merely by recruiting more blacks and other racial minorities into colleges and then into high-paying jobs. This is to assume, simply, that we can solve the problems of racial minorities by elevating them to full partnership in the problems of the racial majority. We assume that when a young black person acquires a degree, puts on a suit, and achieves a sit-down job with a corporation, the problem is to that extent solved.

The larger, graver, more dangerous problem, however, is that we have thought of no better way of solving the race problem. The "success" of the black corporate executive, in fact, only reveals the shallowness, the jeopardy, and the falseness of the "success" of the white corporate executive. This "success" is a private and highly questionable settlement that does not solve, indeed does not refer to, the issues associated with American racism. It only assumes that American blacks will be made better or more useful or more secure by becoming as greedy, selfish, wasteful, and thoughtless as affluent American whites. The aims and standards of the oppressors become the aims and standards of the oppressed, and so our ills and evils survive our successive "liberations."

The problems associated with racism, as I have already suggested, are deeply involved in our national character, and they will not be solved by a racially equitable distribution of college degrees and professional salaries. There are several of these problems, and all of them are difficult. There would be more hope of solving them if they could be understood in such a way as to show the unlikelihood that the solutions can be simple—the unlikelihood, that is, that remedies can be thought up by the people at the top and bestowed or imposed upon the people lower down. To that end, I would like to try my hand at a description of four of these problems as they appear to me.

———

The first problem is the displacement of the racial problem itself from the country to the cities. The story of the black race in America began and went on for more than three hundred years as a story that was mainly rural and agricultural. With the industrialization of agriculture and the increasing availability of factory jobs during and after World War II, the story of American blacks rapidly became an urban one. If all the black emigrants from the countryside had found secure jobs and agreeable dwellings in the cities, their story would, of course, have been a different and a better one. Too often, what they found were poor jobs or no jobs, and deplorable living conditions. The move from country to city, moreover, deprived them of their competence in doing for themselves. It is no exaggeration to say that, in the country, most blacks were skilled in the arts of make-do and subsistence. If most of them were poor, they were *competently* poor; they could do for themselves and for each other. They knew how to grow and harvest and prepare food. They knew how to gather wild fruits, nuts, and herbs. They knew how to hunt and fish. They knew how to use the things that their white "superiors" threw away or disregarded or overlooked. Some of them were becoming capable small landowners. In the cities, all of this know-how was suddenly of no value, and they became abjectly and dependently poor as they never had been before. In the country, despite the limits placed upon them by segregation and poverty, they possessed a certain freedom in their ability to *do* things, but once they were in the city freedom was inescapably associated with the ability to *buy* things.

This loss of the efficacy of competence would be regrettable, indeed dangerous, whatever people it might have happened to (and, of course, it has happened to white people also), but in the story of American blacks it involves a particularly poignant loss of an opportunity for justice. Since blacks had been farm workers throughout their history in America, first as slaves and then as poor sharecroppers or day laborers, the correct and appropriate justice to them would have been to help and encourage them, so far as their individual abilities and desires allowed, to become owners of small farms. This would have been the healing of the wound of slavery that the freed slaves themselves envisioned in their plea for "forty acres and a mule." Instead, they were regarded as "excess population" in the country as soon as they were replaceable by machines, and they moved into the urban slums where, still, they are regarded as "excess population." We have probably dealt with this "excess" as well as we can by moving it around, and that is only to say that we have not dealt with it at all. To deal with it, we have to understand why these people became an "excess" in the first place, and what they and we have lost in the loss of their usefulness. And in order to understand that, we have to understand the abuses, excesses, penalties, and costs of our present ways of farming. We have to understand the substitution of industrial methods and devices for human skill and human labor, and the complex costs of that substitution.

———

One of the costs is dispossession, which is the second problem. In 1920 black American farmers owned 916,000 farms, totaling fifteen million acres. By 1988, according to the New York Times News Service, the number of farms owned by blacks had fallen to 30,000, totaling about three million acres. Congressman Mike Espy of Mississippi says that there were 164,000 black farmers in his state in 1910, and in 1980 there were fewer than 9,000. These figures greatly embarrass some of our conventional assumptions about racism and civil rights. For one thing, the steepest decline in land ownership by blacks, which occurred from 1950 to 1970, coincides roughly with the period of their greatest gains in civil rights. For another, even though the decline of land ownership among blacks has been greater than that among whites, the decline has been precipitous and catastrophic for both races, and for both races the causes have been mostly the same. In the decline of black farming, racial prejudice has, of course, played a significant part. But, beyond that, black farmers have failed or quit because of the same economic, political, and social adversities that have affected white farmers. Black farmers, one gathers, have lost out to a considerable extent not because they were black farmers but because they were small farmers. And it is reasonable to suppose that the black small farmers have not received government help because any measures that would have helped them would also have helped the more numerous white small farmers—thus requiring official sanction for a democratic distribution of usable property.

But at least since the time of the notorious Committee for Economic Development in the early 1940s, our government's policy for rural citizens, hence ultimately for all citizens, has been dispossession: the removal of the vast majority of all races from the independent use or ownership of land or other usable property. The decline of black farmers, then, though it may be attributable to some extent to racial prejudice, is mainly attributable to their being caught up along with white farmers in the much more comprehensive and powerful prejudice against the small landowner.

As a result of this prejudice, nearly our whole population is now dispossessed, and our most populous economic classes are the affluent dispossessed and the impoverished dispossessed. How much more secure the affluent dispossessed will prove to be, in the long run, than the impoverished dispossessed is a question that we are leaving to history to decide. At present, from the point of view of the affluent, dispossession gives the advantage of freedom from the work and worry of taking care of property; the dependency that dispossession also involves is not noticed. From the point of view of the impoverished, the dependency is noticeable immediately; for them, dispossession means, simply, the loss of the ability to help themselves.

———

Thus, moving a problem does not correct it, but makes it much more difficult to correct. With movement, the problem changes. The black slaves and former slaves of a farming economy, whatever their political status, had an economic usefulness and value as workers, and they had in themselves a sure, if limited, competence to help themselves. Their abilities gave them a connection to the productive capacities of the country itself that was not absolutely dependent upon their employers, and those blacks who came to own land were as independent of employers as anyone else who owned land. As competent country people, they were not completely at the mercy of their political or economic condition.

Their descendents, living in the inner-city slums of the 1980s, are no longer legally excluded from the institutions of citizenship, and so their political status may be said to have improved; but their economic status has become more dependent, consumptive, and degraded than it was before. They have no direct connection to the productive capacities of the country itself, hence no ability to perform within the legitimate economy on their own behalf, and many of them are not employed at all. According to *The Washington Spectator* of April 1, 1988, "The unemployment rate among young blacks in Harlem is more than 40 percent." Many in that 40 percent undoubtedly belong to that new American class, the "permanently unemployable." As citizens they have the right to vote and such, but the unemployed and "permanently unemployable" live outside the country's economy, or are merely, so to speak, its patients.

The transition from slave to citizen is good. But the transition from useful and therefore valuable slave to useless and therefore costly economic dependent is a bewilderment. There must be some good in it, but how much of that good is net? There is certainly danger in it, for the unemployed and the "permanently unemployable" and for everyone else. It may prove to be as dangerous for all concerned as slavery was.

And how much sense, after all, does this unemployment make? People are unemployed, for one reason, because they are replaceable by machines that work more cheaply than people (in a time of cheap energy), thus enlarging the profits of the affluent class. And yet no one who has looked can argue that the country is well cared for, either its rural places or its cities. A lot of work needs to be done, work that would help the country and everyone in it, if only it were possible to pay people to do it. Forty percent of the young blacks in

Harlem are unemployed, and yet the crops cannot be harvested in many areas without illegal immigrants from Mexico—two facts that cannot be put together in such a way as to make sense.

We come, then, to this question: How *racially* significant is it that we now have many blacks who have college degrees, wear suits, are members of professions or officers of corporations, if 40 percent of the young black people of Harlem are unemployed? It certainly does not mean that the black *race* is succeeding in this country. It can only mean that the black race is now as divided within and against itself as is the white race. If this is a racial achievement, its significance is not clear to me.

Or what is the racial significance of the affluence of some blacks, when many other blacks are working at the most menial jobs? It would be clearer to say that this phenomenon has an economic significance, and that its economic significance is about the same as that of slavery: as long as there are some people who wish to believe and are economically empowered to believe that they are too good to do their own work and clean up after themselves, then somebody else is going to have to do the work and the cleaning up. In an exploitive economy, there is what we might call a "nigger factor" that will remain more or less constant. If some people grow rich by making things to throw away, then many other people will have to empty the garbage cans and make the trip to the dump.

————

A third problem, therefore, has to do with the extreme doubtfulness of economic solutions made within the terms of an economy based on the exploitation of power, the exhaustion of natural sources, the misuse of people, and the waste of products. What, in the first place, have we gained as a nation by paying high wages to workers for the carting away of our so-called wastes and by paying much higher wages to the corporate executives who are responsible for the existence of those wastes, both kinds of employment being utterly degrading of both humanity and the world? And in the second place, how can blacks be elevated in security or dignity by an "equal" participation in such work and such earning?

In light of the issue of the spiritual health of human beings, the issue of wages may be more or less arbitrary or irrelevant. What would be a just wage for a life of carrying off other people's cans and bottles? A million dollars a year would not be enough, because such a job can be performed only by the forfeiture of the effective life of the spirit in this world. Such work is not, in the usual sense, an accomplishment. It is not productive work. The only conceivable standard for it is quantitative; it can be done thoroughly or not; one can haul off either all the cans and bottles or only some of them. It is work that by its nature cannot be good work; though it can be done carefully, it cannot be well done. There is no art in it, no science, and no skill. Its only virtue is in its necessity. But it is necessary only for a bad reason: the manufacture of "disposable" (that is, virtually worthless) products. The people for whom this work is done will be made unhappy or unhealthy if it is not done. So long as it is done, they will scarcely think of it. It is work, then, that is entirely negative in its value. Its most desirable result is to leave no visible trace.

I said and meant that a million dollars a year would not be enough for such work, and I can easily imagine the outrage with which some readers will respond to that judgment. Why, a million dollars a year is an executive's wages! And an executive, after all, has a college degree, lives in an expensive house, and drives an expensive car. He or she wears a suit and sweats only when jogging (or worrying). Since executives do no manual or menial or domestic work, an executive's body becomes only passively dirty—by its own secretions and by the filth that falls upon it out of the air; it is never soiled by any dust that *it* has raised. Obviously, then, an executive is much superior to a garbage collector. But is this true? Let us see.

An executive, of course, is understood to be a large operator, a person of the big-time. A small businessman or businesswoman, the owner of a small independent store or shop, will not think him- or herself, or be thought, an executive. Such people *do*; they do not "execute." The executive deals in large quantities of products which, typically, are purchased as cheaply as possible, and sold as dearly as possible. Typically, the products are never touched by the executive, and they come from and go to people and places the executive does not know, or care about, or give any respect or allegiance to. Many of those products are not necessary. Many of them are overpriced. Many of them cause environmental or social or cultural damage. Many of them are destroyed quickly in use but remain indestructible as garbage or pollutants. Many of them are shoddily made. Many executives grow rich by the manufacture and sale of products that, being rich, they disdain to use. All of them grow rich by work that they do not do, and would disdain to do.

The work of the executive is thus as unproductive and as spiritually desolate as that of the garbage collector. Indeed, depending upon the toxicity and persistence of the products and by-products, it may be more so. Certainly, by any standard, to haul garbage away is more virtuous than to manufacture it.

What all of us—black and white—must understand is that the existence of industrial executives, as we now have them, implies inevitably the "nigger work" of garbage collectors and other menial laborers, as we now have them. The career of the black executive implies just as much "nigger work" as the career of the white executive. And the degradation of this trade in careers and souls is not limited to people. For the garbage cannot be hauled out of the world; it must be *put* somewhere. The inevitably misnamed "sanitary landfills" were once places of dignity, woodlands or marshes or farms, the homes of creatures, and now they have been made niggers also.

Nor is that the end of it. The existence of the typical corporate executive, black or white, implies inevitably not just the "nigger work" of cleaning up after other people, and the niggerfication of the people, black or white, who must deal with the messes, and of the places where the messes are hidden away; it implies also the unemployed young people and the "permanently unemployable" of the urban ghettos, who do not have the dignity even of "nigger work." The willingness to profit from a destructive economy at the top results in economic nonentity at the bottom. Economic nonentity, as we know, is a condition that people grow extremely tired of, and when tired of it become extremely dangerous.

———

But even from the most selfish point of view, the success of the typical executive, black or white, is not very successful, and his or her security is not very secure. For one thing, this success and security can be achieved only by investing one's life in an economy that is destroying its natural sources and therefore itself as surely as water runs downhill. For another, this personal success and security, which are usually involved in the success and security of a corporation, in no way involve the success and security of society. The terms of this success and security are individualistic and competitive. The executive, that is, takes what he or she can get by the use of whatever power is available, just as the garbage collector does. The process of gaining this success and security thus isolates the individual both from nature and from other humans—which, of course, is a description of failure and insecurity.

There are two ways by which individual success and security can be made (within mortal limits) successful and secure: they must rest on a sound understanding and practice of economic justice; and they must involve and be involved in the success and security of the community. The competitive principle excludes both of these ways.

We might as well admit that we do not have a working concept of economic justice. We are resigned to the poor principle that people earn what they earn by power, not by the quality or usefulness of their work. Insurance executives, doctors, lawyers, mechanics, factory workers, and garbage collectors all earn in proportion to their power. People such as the small farmers, who have no power, must resign themselves to earning what they can get. This is what we mean by our understanding that the market is the ultimate arbiter of economic values. Workers will not be paid according to the quality of their work or their products, but according to their power. The market is thus detached utterly from the issue of quality and made utterly subject to manipulation by the most powerful in their own interest.

The first principle of economic justice, however, is that good work will be well paid. It follows that the first necessity of economic justice is good work—something that we, as a nation, are less and less capable of doing. The market as a mere brokerage of economic power—apart from the principled high standards of the seller and the discriminating judgment of the buyer—will inevitably have a degenerative influence on both the quality of people and the quality of products.

But surely we must go even farther and say that a market will be degenerative if it is not under the rule of the virtues. The most obvious lesson of slavery, one that we have never learned, is about the limits of a mere market. A mere market cannot adequately recognize or protect the full value of a creature, as seller or as buyer or as merchandise. We now call a market "free" to the extent that buyers and sellers are able to ignore this limitation. But it was a limit not ignorable by slaves or by the enemies of slavery. To them it was plain that the market was inevitably reductive: it treated people as bodies, not as souls.

We cannot now legally own the body of another person. And yet our market for labor, as for things, is more crudely reductive now than it was then. Slaves at least were priced according to their qualities and abilities, whereas now workers, in both the trades and the professions, are more and more likely to receive "the going rate," regardless of their competence. And now their work, whether physical or mental, is likely to be more degrading spiritually than the work of skilled slaves. This, paradoxically, is the result of the market's general depreciation of all physical and material things. For we have kept institutionalized in our economic system a dualism much like the dualism that justified and enforced slavery. Despite the physical force that it requires, a slave economy is under the domination of mind. Any healthy body, as we know, is able to do the work necessary for its own maintenance. It was the mind of the master, not his body, that required the service of a slave. The slave subserved an economic idea.

Work, in our own day, is on the same terms increasingly slavish, because our economy is more mind-dominated now than it was in the time of slavery, and is increasingly so. As I have already suggested, it is not necessary for executives ever to touch either the raw material or the manufactured product by which they earn money. The work of executives is entirely mental; their physical lives are artificial, given to purely consumptive activities like golf and jogging.

And the work of the tradesman or laborer or factory worker, though it deals with material things, tends to be as mind-dominated and abstract as that of the executive. The industrial laborer subserves an economic idea instituted in machines and in mechanized procedures. This is as far as possible from the work of the traditional craftsman or artist, whose making has never resembled what we now call "manufacture," but is a cooperation and conversation of mind and body and idea and material. The true craftsman does not waste materials because his or her art involves respect for materials. And the craftsman's products are not wasted because by their quality and durability they earn respect.

A dualistic society dominated by mind involves a number of dangers, of which the degradation and destruction of the material world is only the most obvious.

It is not so obvious, or so expectable, that in a mind-dominated society, fewer and fewer people will possess independently the power or ability to make up their own minds. This is because dominance of mind always implies, politically and economically, dominance by somebody else's mind—or, worse, by the "mind" of a government or corporation.

In a society in which nearly everybody is dominated by somebody else's mind or by a disembodied mind, it becomes increasingly difficult to learn the truth about the activities of governments and corporations, about the quality or value of products, or about the health of one's own place and economy.

In such a society, also, our private economies will depend less and less upon the private ownership of real, usable property, and more and more upon property that is institutional and abstract, beyond individual control, such as money, insurance policies, certificates of deposit, stocks, and shares. And as our private economies become more abstract, the mutual, free helps and pleasures of family and community life will be supplanted by a kind of displaced or placeless citizenship and by commerce with impersonal and self-interested suppliers.

All of us, in fact, are now involved in destructive work or destructive pleasure or both. All of us are now directly dependent, economically and politically, upon the minds and ideas of people whom we do not know. Most of us have no way of knowing except, too late, by scandal or disaster, what is going on in the governments and the corporations. Most of us own no usable property. Most of us are watching the dispersal or disintegration of our families and communities.

Thus, although we are not slaves in name, and cannot be carried to market and sold as somebody else's legal chattels, we are free only within narrow limits. For all our talk about liberation and personal autonomy, there are few choices that we are free to make. What would be the point, for example, if a majority of our people decided to be self-employed?

The great enemy of freedom is the alignment of political power with wealth. This alignment destroys the commonwealth—that is, the natural wealth of localities and the local economies of household, neighborhood, and community—and so destroys democracy, of which the commonwealth is the foundation and the practical means. This happens—it is happening—because the alignment of wealth and power permits economic value to overturn value of any other kind. The value of everything is reduced to its market price. A thing not marketable has no value. It is increasingly apparent that we cannot value things except by selling them, and that we think it acceptable, and indeed respectable, to sell anything. For a number of years now the ruling political idea in my home state has been "Sell Kentucky." We speak more and more easily, too, of "selling" ideas. It is harder all the time to affirm the existence, or the right to exist, of a thing or an idea that "won't sell." Indeed, it is increasingly evident that we have replaced the old market on which people were sold with a new market on which people sell themselves.

Several months ago I attended the commencement exercises of a California university at which the graduates of the school of business wore "For Sale" signs around their necks. It was done as a joke, of course, a display of youthful high spirits, and yet it was inescapably a cynical joke, of the sort by which an embarrassing truth is flaunted. For, in fact, these graduates were for sale, they knew that they were, and they intended to be. They had just spent four years at a university to increase their "marketability." That some of the young women in the group undoubtedly were feminists only made the joke more cynical. But what most astonished and alarmed me was that a number of these graduates for sale were black. Had their forebears served and suffered and struggled in America for 368 years in order for these now certified and privileged few to sell themselves? Did they not know that only 122 years, two lifetimes, ago, their forebears had worn in effect that very sign? It seemed to me that I was witnessing the tragedy of history that the forgetfulness of history always is—and a tragedy not for blacks alone. If the people among us who know best, or ought to, what it means to be sold come to forget it or ignore it so far as to sell themselves, what is to become of the rest of us? If *they* have not learned better, how will the rest of us learn?

How, remembering their history, could those black graduates have worn those signs? Only, I think, by assuming, in very dangerous innocence, that their graduation into privilege exempted them from history. The danger is that there is no safety, no *dependable* safety, in privilege that is founded on greed, ignorance, and waste.

And these people, after all, will remain black. What sign will they wear besides their expensive suits by which the police can tell them from their unemployed and unemployable brothers and sisters of the inner city?

––––––

There is no safety in belonging to the select few, for minority people or anybody else. If we are looking for insurance against want and oppression, we will find it only in our neighbors' prosperity and goodwill and, beyond that, in the good health of our worldly places, our homelands. If we were sincerely looking for a place of safety, for real security and success, then we would begin to turn to our communities—and not the communities simply of our human neighbors, but also of the water, earth, and air, the plants and animals, all the creatures with whom our local life is shared. We would be looking too for another kind of freedom. Our present idea of freedom is only the freedom to do as we please: to sell ourselves for a high salary, a home in the suburbs, and idle weekends. But that is a freedom dependent upon affluence, which is in turn dependent upon the rapid consumption of exhaustible supplies. The other kind of freedom is the freedom to take care of ourselves and of each other. The freedom of affluence opposes and contradicts the freedom of community life.

Our place of safety can only be the community, and not just one community, but many of them everywhere. Upon that depends all that we still claim to value: freedom, dignity, health, mutual help and affection, undestructive pleasure, and the rest. Human life, as most of us still would like to define it, is community life. And this brings me to the fourth problem, and the last, that I want to consider: How can "integration" be achieved—and what can it mean—in communities that are conspicuously disintegrating?

In a "Face to Face" television interview on July 8, 1967, Roy Wilkins described this problem pointedly enough:

> In the South we still have a great deal of Negro family stability and control, and community control of families, and the imposition of standards of conduct. In the North, with its great anonymous cities, Negro families come there, sometimes they're disintegrated—but even where they're not, they are lost in a huge population; the minister doesn't keep tabs on them like the minister did in the small town back home; they don't know the police chief, and they don't care, and they don't know the judge and they don't know the things and the controls that operated in their home community. And when they come to Harlem, they're just "John Smith," and they can do as they please. They don't have to pay any attention to Mom and Pop, and the minister and the neighbor, or anybody who knows about them and helps to control them. So they run wild, some of them; others busy themselves going to night school and doing all the things that other people do.

With a few small differences, that describes a tragedy that is as white as it is black. The gravity of the problem is suggested by the fact that the disintegration Wilkins described coincides neatly with what a great many people, black and white, understand as freedom. People who wish to be free to pay no attention to anybody who knows them are not going to accept the constraints or pursue the freedoms of community life. They accept disintegration as the price or the sign of "success." Like the for-sale graduates of the California university, they think that mockery of history is "sophistication."

Mostly, we do not speak of our society as disintegrating. We would prefer not to call what we are experiencing social disintegration. But we are endlessly preoccupied with the symptoms: divorce, venereal disease, murder, rape, debt, bankruptcy, pornography, soil loss, teenage pregnancy, fatherless children, motherless children, child suicide, public child-care, retirement homes, nursing homes, toxic waste, soil and water and air pollution, government secrecy, government lying, government crime, civil violence, drug abuse, sexual promiscuity, abortion as "birth control," the explosion of garbage, hopeless poverty, unemployment, unearned wealth. We know the symptoms well enough. All the plagues of our time are symptoms of a general disintegration.

We are capable, really, only of the forcible integration of centralization—economic, political, military, and educational—and always at the cost of social and cultural disintegration. Our aim, it would appear, is to "integrate" ourselves into a limitless military-industrial city in which we all will be lost, and so may do as we please in the freedom either to run wild until we are caught or killed, or to do "all the things that other people do."

That we prefer to deal piecemeal with the problems of disintegration keeps them "newsworthy" and profitable to the sellers of cures. To see them as merely the symptoms of a greater problem would require hard thought, a change of heart, and a search for the fundamental causes.

Drug abuse, for example, will remain an easy political cause, and a lucrative business for everybody but the victims, so long as we take refuge in our meaningless distinction between legal and illegal drugs. How can we hope to stop the distribution of drugs in "the drug world" so long as we are unconcerned about the distribution of drugs by the drugstore? In fact, people use drugs, legal and illegal, because their lives are intolerably painful or dull. They hate their work and find no rest in their leisure. They are estranged from

their families and their neighbors. It should tell us something that in
healthy societies drug use is celebrative, convivial, and occasional,
whereas among us it is lonely, shameful, and addictive. We need
drugs, apparently, because we have lost each other.

————————

But surely the most poignant symptom of disintegration is "integration" by the forced busing of schoolchildren to "achieve racial
balance in the schools." This is an extremely risky subject for a
white person to talk about because busing has become the major
tool of integration, and so has taken on great force as a political
symbol. Only a racist, it is assumed, can oppose busing for racial
balance.

There are, nevertheless, some things about this practice that are
wrong. For one thing, by focusing exclusively on the issue of racial
balance in the schools, busing tends to distract attention from the
much more widespread phenomenon of segregation by economic
subdivision. I mean the division of urban and suburban economic
classes—poor, blue collar, professional, very rich—into separate
ghettos or enclaves. And this economic division is fractioned even
more by the tendency of professional people and intellectuals to co-
here in widely dispersed "networks," often to the virtual exclusion
of community ties. Many people now feel more at home, and more
at ease socially, at a professional convention than in the streets of
their own neighborhood. But as the "successful" abandon the communities that they once shared with the unsuccessful, they forget
the unsuccessful and leave them without examples or defenders.
The children of the unsuccessful then have no models, or they have
models only of the worst kind.

There are reasons for this economic segregation or disintegration, of course, and chief among them are economic and insti-

tutional centralization—and the automobile and TV, which are the technology of centralization. People don't work or shop or amuse themselves or go to church or school in their own neighborhoods anymore, and are therefore free to separate themselves from their work places and economic sources, and to sort themselves into economic categories in which, having no need for each other, they remain strangers. I assume that this is bad because I assume that it is good for people to know each other. I assume, especially, that it is good for people to know each other across the lines of economy and vocation. Professional people should know their clients outside their offices. Teachers should know the families of their students. University professors and intellectuals should know the communities and the households that will be affected by their ideas. Rich people and poor people should know each other. If this familiar knowledge does not exist, then these various groups will think of each other and deal with each other on the basis of stereotypes as vicious and ultimately as dangerous as the stereotypes of race.

It is in connection with this larger disintegration that busing for integration must be thought about, for busing (for school consolidation) was a tool of the larger disintegration long before it became a tool of racial integration.

My own children were bused to school from the first grade on. Their daily bus ride to and from school took about two hours of every day. This meant that they were under school discipline—expected to sit still, etc.—about a third again as long each day as their schoolmates in town. It also meant that they were under home discipline two hours a day less than the town children; they had that much less time for chores, homework, and free play. In my opinion, all this bus travel was damaging to the lives of my children both at school and at home. Moreover, the grade school that my children attended was nine miles, and their middle and high schools twelve miles, from home, well beyond the range of close or easy parental involvement. School consolidation thus involves a great expense of time and money that might be better spent in the education and up-bringing of children.

Thus the question that I have had to ask myself out of my own experience is this: How can I be for busing as a tool of integration, when I am against it as a tool of consolidation? My own experience suggests to me that busing for any reason is, in reality, a tool of dis-integration. I believe in neighborhood schools for the same reasons that I believe in neighborhood shops and stores, for the same reasons that I believe in neighborhood.

There can be no greater blow to the integrity of a community than the loss of its school or loss of control of its school—which always means loss of control of its children. The breakdown of discipline and academic standards in the schools can only originate in, and can only cause, the breakdown of community life. The public school, separated from the community by busing (for whatever reason), government control, consolidation, and other "advances," has become a no-man's-land, a place existing in reference only to itself and to a theoretical "tomorrow's world." Neither teachers nor students feel themselves answerable to the community, for the school does not exist to serve the community. It exists to aid and abet the student's escape from the community into "tomorrow's world," in which community standards, it goes without saying, will not apply. The teachers are divided from the community by the shibboleths of "professional training," "professional standards," and "academic freedom." The students are divided from the community by the distance of school from home, by parental indifference to the affairs of a distant school not under their influence or control, and by changes in curriculum or teaching methods that make it impossible for many of them to get help from their elders. Teachers who are preparing students for jobs in "tomorrow's world," without reference to the local community or community anywhere, need not be surprised if their efforts are not enthusiastically affirmed by parents who are, after all, living in today's world.

The longer these imposed-from-above "solutions" continue, the more unsatisfactory they will prove to be. It is impossible to believe that people can be changed fundamentally by government requirement. People do not pay taxes voluntarily, for example, and they will not learn to do so in a thousand years of involuntary taxpaying. The only thing that a government requirement assures is a prolongation of government supervision. It is certain that the government should forbid racial injustice to the same extent that it should forbid injustice of any other kind. But that interracial liking and harmony can be the result of a government program is extremely doubtful. One may reasonably suspect, indeed, that government programs of social amelioration, such as welfare and busing, exist as poor apologies for the government's espousal of the economic and technological determinism that has virtually destroyed community life and community economy everywhere in the country.

A true and appropriate answer to our race problem, as to many others, would be a restoration of our communities—it being understood that a community, properly speaking, cannot exclude or mistreat any of its members. This is what we forgot during slavery and the industrialization that followed, and have never remembered. A proper community, we should remember also, is a commonwealth: a place, a resource, and an economy. It answers the needs, practical as well as social and spiritual, of its members— among them the need to need one another. The answer to the present alignment of political power with wealth is the restoration of the identity of community and economy.

Is this something that the government could help with? Of course it is. Community cannot be made by government prescription and mandate, but the government, in its proper role as promoter of the general welfare, preserver of the public peace, and forbidder of injustice, could do much to promote the improvement of communities. If it wanted to, it could end its collusion with the wealthy and the corporations and the "special interests." It could stand, as it is supposed to, between wealth and power. It could assure the possibility that a poor person might hold office. It could protect, by strict forbiddings, the disruption of the integrity of a community or a local economy or an ecosystem by any sort of commercial or industrial enterprise, that is, it could enforce proprieties of scale. It could understand that economic justice does not consist in giving the most power to the most money.

The government *could* do such things. But we know well that it is not going to do them; it is not even going to consider doing them, because community integrity, and the decentralization of power and economy that it implies, is antithetical to the ambitions of the corporations. The government's aim, therefore, is racial indifference, not integrated communities. Does this mean that our predicament is hopeless? No. It only means that our predicament is extremely unfavorable, as the human predicament has often been.

What the government will or will not do is finally beside the point. If people do not have the government they want, then they will have a government that they must either change or endure. Finally, all the issues that I have discussed here are neither political nor economic, but moral and spiritual. What is at issue is our character as a people. It is necessary to look beyond the government to the possibility—one that seems to be growing—that people will reject what have been the prevailing assumptions, and begin to strengthen and defend their communities on their own.

We must be aware too of the certainty that the present way of things will eventually fail. If it fails quickly, by any of several predicted causes, then we will have no need, being absent, to worry about what to do next. If it fails slowly, and if we have been careful to preserve the most necessary and valuable things, then it may fail into a restoration of community life—that is, into understanding of our need to help and comfort each other.

Port Royal, Kentucky
Summer 1988